HOLY BAPTISM
Two Writings on the Sacrament

By Charles Porterfield Krauth

www.JustandSinner.com

Infant Baptism and Infant Salvation in the
Calvinistic System

A Review of Dr. Hodge's Systematic Theology
By Charles Porterfield Krauth

Original Publishing Info:
PHILADELPHIA:
LUTHERAN BOOK STORE, 117 N. SIXTH STREET
1874

HOLY BAPTISM

INCLUDING:
INFANT BAPTISM AND INFANT SALVATION IN
THE CALVINISTIC SYSTEM
And
BAPTISM: THE DOCTRINE SET FORTH IN HOLY
SCRIPTURE AND TAUGHT IN THE
EVANGELICAL LUTHERAN CHURCH
By Charles Porterfield Krauth

Just & Sinner
425 East Lincoln Ave.
Watseka, IL 60970

www.JustandSinner.com

ISBN 10: 0692465790
ISBN 13: 978-0692465790

TABLE OF CONTENTS

§1. OUTLINE AND GENERAL ESTIMATE OF DR. HODGE'S SYSTEMATIC THEOLOGY.

The work opens with an Introduction, which treats of Method; Theology; Rationalism; Mysticism; the Rule of Faith in the Roman Catholic and Protestant view.

The First Part embraces Theology proper; under which are treated: Origin of the idea of God; Theism; Antitheistic Theories; Knowledge of God; His Nature and Attributes; the Trinity; Divinity of Christ; the Holy Spirit; the Decree of God; Creation; Providence; Miracles; Angels.

The Second Part is occupied with Anthropology: Man, his Origin and Nature; Origin of the Soul; Unity of the Human Race; Original State of Man; Covenant of Works; the Fall; Sin; Free Agency.

The Third Part presents Soteriology: the Plan of Salvation; Covenant of Grace; the Person of Christ; His Mediatorial Work; Prophetic and Priestly Offices; Satisfaction-; for Whom did Christ Die? Theories of the Atonement; Christ's Intercession; Kingly Office; Humiliation; Exaltation; Vocation; Regeneration; Faith; Justification; Sanctification; the Law, with a Particular Commentary on each Commandment; the Means of Grace; the Word of God; the Sacraments; Baptism; the Lord's Supper; Prayer.

The Fourth Part is Eschatology: The State of the Soul after Death; Resurrection; Second Advent; Concomitants of the Second Advent.

Of the general fullness and logical order of this arrangement there can be no question. The discussion of the Divinity of Christ as distinct from the Trinity might perhaps better have been given under Soteriology, so as not to separate the "Divinity of Christ" from the "Person of Christ." The most important defect in the plan is that it does not embrace a distinct and full treatment of the doctrine concerning the Church. The omission has been made for some reason which satisfies Dr. Hodge. We hope that it means that he proposes to give to the Church a monograph on this subject, one of the most vitally important and interesting doctrines at all times, but especially in our own day. We know of no man more competent than Dr. Hodge to rebuke, with the effectual weapons of fact and logic, the insane pretenses of the rampant pseudo ecclesiasticism of our time, and the yet insaner radicalism, which frightens many into the ecclesiasticism.

The first thing which strikes us in reading Dr. Hodge's book is the style. Whether we shall accept or reject what he maintains may sometimes involve a question, or a pause; but his simple, luminous mode of statement rarely leaves us in any embarrassment as to what it is on which we are to decide. The sentences are never involved. The language is a model of clearness. There is a plain solid sense, the result of a sound judgment thoroughly matured, which is delightful beyond expression in this day and land of fine writing. This, of course, will expose Dr. Hodge to the charge of shallowness, from those who think that nothing is deep but what is unintelligible, and that the art of good writing is the art of putting words to things in the proportion of Falstaff's sack to Falstaff's bread, and that the measure of words is like the measure of Falstaff in the girth.

Another great feature of Dr. Hodge's book is, its value to our common Christianity—nay, in a wide sense, to religion on that broader definition in which the believing Jew has a common interest with the

Christian. To the gratitude of Jew and Christian, Dr.
Hodge is entitled by the able vindication of Revelation
against the assaults which would bring the faith of Jew
and Christian alike to the dust. To Roman Catholic and
Protestant, Dr. Hodge comes with a defense of the
common creeds of Christendom; to Calvinist and
Lutheran, with the able argument on the distinctive
elements of Protestantism and the precious truths
reasserted by the original Churches of the Reformation.
Even in its relative isolation as distinctively Calvinistic,
Dr. Hodge's book is invaluable. It is the gauge of the
type of Calvinism which is considered by its ablest
living representatives as tenable; a Calvinism so gentle
in its spirit toward other forms of evangelical
Christianity, and so full of the disposition to mitigate its
own harder points, as to furnish irenical elements of
the most hopeful kind.

The general mildness, fairness, and clearness of
the book are beyond dispute. It treats Polemics in the
spirit of Irenics, for the most part, but with here and
there a delightful little dash of merited sarcasm, a
suspicion of irony, a playful contempt for small
presumption, and a quiet smile at the absurd, which
humanize the argument, and, with those touches which
make the whole world kin, bring the author nearer to
the reader. Nor are there wanting earnest and eloquent
passages, which deal with sin in a manner in keeping
with its exceeding sinfullness, and with conscious
perversions after their evil deserts. There is no amiable
inanity in the book. It is not done in water-colors, as
some people would think it must be, because it is not
executed with a red-hot poker on an oak-board. Yet its
prevailing character is mild, quiet, firm, judicial. If it is
often pleading, it is still more frequently the decision of
a judge, who sums up evidence, interprets the law, and
pronounces the sentence.

The evidences of enormous, yet reflective,

reading everywhere present themselves, reading of the most varied kind, among the best books and the worst books. There is a gathering of honey for stores, and of poisons for the study of antidotes. The range stretches over the ages, takes in largely the German theology, and reaches apparently almost to the days in which the volumes have come from the press. The result of this anxiety to bring things down to the hour has necessarily been that some of the latest reading has been hasty and has involved Dr. Hodge in mistakes. But the Doctor's greatest weakness, in this immensity of reading, is where it might least have been suspected—it is in Calvinistic theology. He seems to have neglected a part of the Calvinistic theologians of no inconsiderable number and bulk. On his own confession, so far as his memory can recall, he has failed to have seen a single one of a very large and influential portion of those divines, so large in fact that for some two centuries it is hard to find one who does not belong to it. But we account for this on the principles of a latent elective affinity. Like seeks only its like and holds it. There rise up in history the grim and grisly features of those old divines who liked election but who loved reprobation; who conceived of the human race as created chiefly as fuel for Tophet,—divines who would have thought nothing of the perdition of a universe or two, and, if necessary, of throwing themselves in, if their logic proved that it was all for God's greater glory—those inexorable Jonahs on whom a wilderness of gourds would have been lost in the attempt to reconcile them to the sparing of Nineveh. If Dr. Hodge long ago encountered these divines, he quietly turned away into his own brighter path, with other visions of the divine glory. He did not plunge into the Sahara, in the possibility of finding an oasis. Penetrated, as all his works show, with the completest recognition which is possible to Calvinism, that God is love, Calvinism itself is hardly in sharper contrast with Lutheranism than, within Calvinism, Dr. Hodge himself is with Gomarus and his pitiless school. The only apology which can be made for that school is that which they constantly make for themselves—that the logic of the system is with them, and that they are with the logic of the system. They did not create the horrors, they only told of them.

The general tone of the book is profoundly devout. Though Dr. Hodge has moved largely and freely in the living world, his most marked affinities are yet with the old. He saith "the old is better." He has not put enough of the new wine into the old bottles to rend them—except perhaps in a spot or two. In spite of recent reading, and of the space devoted to the callow heresies of the hour, the conception and organism of the book is prevailingly scholastic, of the old Protestant type. It is old-fashioned theology in the main; and, like the best old-fashioned theology, it has the heart of living piety beating through it. It is not satisfied with teaching *about* theology: it teaches theology, it is theology—a true "*theologia egenitorum.*" Its solid judgment and learning will mark it to scholars as one of the classics of Calvinistic Dogmatics, the ablest work in its specific department in English literature. But it is more than this, better than this. The graces of Christian life are not repressed in it, as they have often been in the arid formulating of systems. Moliere's Mock Doctor claimed no more than that the medical profession had changed the place of the heart from the left side to the right; some of the doctors in theology have left the heart out altogether. But in Dr. Hodge's Body of Divinity there is a heart whose beat is that of the fullest health—and you can touch the system nowhere without feeling a pulse. It is a book for the affections. No man could obtrude himself less in his books than Dr. Hodge does; yet all the more for this very reason do we see the man himself in his books. His life has been shaped upon the advice of old Sir John Davies:

"Study the best and highest things that are;
But of thyself, an humble thought retain."

Dr. Hodge's system furnishes a general landmark for Christian thinking in one of its most influential shapes; it also furnishes a revelation of the spirit of Christian science, a picture of the Christian scholar, a miniature of the Christian life. Dr. Hodge constitutes in himself a distinct evidence of Christianity, and alike in what he writes and what he is, vindicates the supremacy of Protestant culture.

§2. INFANTS, INFANT BAPTISM, AND INFANT SALVATION IN THE CALVINISTIC SYSTEM.

It is a marked feature in Dr. Hodge's book that it does unusual justice to the relative importance of Lutheran theology. There are but two developed systems in the world that claim with any show of probability to be purely Biblical. These systems are the Lutheran and the Calvinistic. They possess a common basis in their recognition of the same rule of faith; their profession of the Old Catholic faith as set forth in the three General Creeds; in their acknowledgment of the doctrine of justification by faith and of its great associated doctrines; and they have vast interests, great stakes, mighty bonds of sympathy in common. No two bodies of Christians have more reason for thoroughly understanding each other than Calvinists and Lutherans have, and no two parts of Christendom are closer together in some vital respects than consistent Calvinism and consistent Lutheranism. It is well worth their while to compare views.

But Dr. Hodge is not only full in his notices of Lutheran theology—he is also fair. Mistakes he has made, and very important ones; but designed misrepresentations he has never made. Next to having Dr. Hodge on one's side is the pleasure of having him as an antagonist; for where conscientious men must discuss a subject, who can express the comfort of honorable, magnanimous dealing on both sides—the feeling that in battling with each other they are also battling for each other, in that grand warfare whose final issue will be what all good men desire, the establishment of truth?

§ 3. THE WESTMINSTER CONFESSION AND ELECT INFANTS.

On various points Dr. Hodge argues against the Lutheran doctrine, or what he believes to be such. One of these points

Baptism. On the "necessity" of Baptism, Dr. Hodge thinks the Lutheran divines have "softened down." On this point he is mistaken. Our divines, beginning with Luther and Melanchthon, have held, and hold to this hour, that Baptism is ordinarily, but not absolutely, necessary. (See Conservative Reformation, pp. 427, seq., 557, seq.) In a note (Vol. III. 605), Dr. Hodge says: "We are sorry to see that Dr. Krauth labors to prove that the Westminster Confession teaches that only a certain part, or some of those, who die in infancy are saved; this he does by putting his own construction on the language of that Confession. We can only say that we never saw a Calvinistic theologian who held that doctrine. We are not learned enough to venture the assertion that no Calvinist ever held it; but if all Calvinists are responsible for what every Calvinist has ever said, and all Lutherans are responsible for everything Luther or Lutherans have ever said, then Dr. Krauth, as well as ourselves, will have a heavy burden to carry."

We say in all sincerity that we should prefer that Dr. Hodge should be right on the question here involved. We wish that the Westminster Confession could be harmonized with the view, that all who die in infancy are certainly saved. We wish we could be brought even fairly to doubt that its teachings are irreconcilable with such a view. We should be glad to have it shown that it is merely our mistaken construction of the Confession which is at fault, and that the meaning of its words, on the principles of correct interpretation, is not what we have supposed. But we have seen what Dr. Hodge "never saw." We have seen more than one Calvinistic theologian who does hold that doctrine. We humbly and utterly deprecate the position in which Dr. Hodge would seem to insist on putting us, if we venture to assert that some Calvinists do hold it, as if it were between him and us a question of sufficient learning, as if the question were, do we know more about Calvinistic theology than Dr. Hodge does? Dr. Hodge has gone over the world of theological literature as few men have done. We acknowledge and reverence in him one of the greatest and ripest scholars of our age; but Apelles acknowledges that a cobbler may be authority on a sandal. And what we shall offer in this effort to show that we are not mistaken in our judgment of Calvinistic teaching, shall be offered with the desire not fairly to offend against the canon: "*Ne sutor ultra.*"

§4. HOW ARE CONFESSIONS TO BE INTERPRETED?

We have certainly said nothing to justify the imputation that we think that every Calvinist is responsible for what every other Calvinist says. The caveat of Dr. Hodge must have reference to what he supposes we would say in defending our position—to wit, that it is supported by the opinion of Calvinistic theologians whom we may have seen, though he has not. But we do not intend to take any line of defense open to the very just objection which Dr. Hodge makes. Our line of defense is this: The Confession has one sense only; this sense is to be fixed by the acknowledged principles of interpretation; the natural sense of the words, as they impress the minds of readers, is, *cœteris paribus*, to be accepted in preference to any other; in case of dispute as to their meaning, the different parts of the Confession are to be compared with reference to the light they shed on each other; if opinions still differ as to the sense, the usage of the authors of the Confession, of the great divines of the Church, and of their successors, the official and sworn teachers and defenders of its faith, are to be appealed to, to show how the words were understood by those who used them, by those who subscribed them, and by the Church in general—and what is the sense most in harmony with the logical necessities and completeness of the system, as its defenders themselves have understood them. A sense fixed by these processes carries with it a moral probability which throws the whole burden of proof on those who deny this sense; they must admit this sense, or demonstrate its incorrectness. We acknowledge that a Church is to be judged by its standards, and not by its divines, as they add to, take from, or change the standards. The Confessions of Churches ought to be guardians of its liberties as well as protectors of its purity. But we cannot judge a Church by its standards unless we have right modes of interpreting the standards. The standards can neither conserve the freedom nor the purity of the Church unless we can settle their true sense, over against the severity which puts into them what they do not mean, and the laxity which takes out of them what they do mean.

Such indeed is the moral force of the utterances of the authors and representative men of Church Confessions, that it is sometimes urged as more than counterbalancing what would be, apart from it, a natural sense of the Confession. On this principle the great Calvinistic Synod of Dort,[1] after conceding that "the words of the third Article of the Arminians, as they outwardly sound and lie before us, seem to be good and orthodox," goes on to say: "but inasmuch as—thus Chrysostom long ago said—the heresy is wont to be in the meaning of the word, the meaning of these words is to be determined, and that from the writings and books of the Remonstrants themselves." With its proper restriction this principle holds good. A confession that punishments are "eternal" if those who make it are avowed Universalists, has its sense fixed by that fact. A confession that Christ is "divine" means little if Socinians make it. There is hardly a page of Dr. Hodge's three volumes which does not assume the correctness of this principle, alike in determining the views held by other Churches, and in establishing his own. It is on the basis of the moral probability of concurrent testimony that he constantly and properly assumes that he has the ability to present a correct interpretation of the Calvinistic system. Throughout he takes the very means, and the only means, we propose to employ, in settling in disputed cases the precise meaning of the Confession of his own Church, and of other Churches. We propose no test for Calvinism which we are not willing to apply to Lutheranism. If we put a sense on our Confession which Dr. Hodge can prove to be in conflict with the views held at the time of its framing by its authors, and out of harmony with the other parts of the system, if we shall define words in it in a sense in which he can show its authors did not use them, and in which they were not received by the line of witnesses who are acknowledged to have been loyal to the faith of the Church, then shall we justify

---

[1] Actor. Part 2, dog. ad Artic. III., p. 261. Ed. Dort.

Dr. Hodge in asserting that we have reached that sense by putting our own construction on its language. But, on the other hand, if we shall fix, on these principles, a certain sense on the familiar terms of Calvinistic Confessions and systems, we shall feel that Dr. Hodge in denying that sense is thrown completely on the defensive, and is bound to show that his denial does not rest on his own construction, a construction reached without the natural aids which history brings to grammar in the interpretation of language.

We rejoice that for himself Dr. Hodge so unequivocally takes ground against the whole dark theory of infant damnation. If he be right in asserting that it never follows from the Calvinistic system, we are glad that the system itself is relieved from the blot; if he be mistaken in this assertion, we rejoice still that the Calvinism of the present is yielding; we rejoice the more because we believe that in yielding this, the old historically defined system yields itself; for we believe, and propose to show, that logical Calvinism is involved in a hopeless entanglement in the whole matter of infant salvation and infant Baptism.

§ 5. THE SALVATION OF INFANTS DEPENDENT ON ABSOLUTE PERSONAL ELECTION.

The Calvinistic system places the salvation of infants on the ground of a divine election of individuals.

HEIDEGGER.[2]—"To those (the elect), who die in infancy, Baptism seals the grace of regeneration... It cannot be doubted, that the souls of *elect infants* dying in infancy, are inserted by the Spirit, into Christ, either before Baptism or at least in Baptism... The Baptism of *elect infants*, is not an empty figure... The *elect infants* receive the seal."

---

[2] Corpus Theologiae: II. 449.

WITSIUS.[3]—"Christ hath not made satisfaction for any sin which He has not taken on Himself. He has taken no sins on Himself except those of the elect. The remission of original sin by the blood of Christ has been obtained for none except for him who is elect." "To the Orthodox, disputing of the efficacy of Baptism, the main, if not the sole inquiry, is, what does it confer on *elect infants, who alone*, according to the strictness of the Divine judgment, *have a right to it (quibus solis ad eum jus est)*?" "By Baptism the good things of the covenant are signed and sealed to *elect infants* as things belonging to them."

WESTMINSTER CONFESSION.[4] —"The grace promised" (in Baptism) is conferred by the Holy Spirit, to such (whether of age or infants) as *that grace belongeth unto, according to the counsel of God's own will.*"

§ 6. INFANTS ELECT AND REPROBATE.

For the Calvinistic system distinctly recognizes "*elect infants*" and thus always virtually, and often in terms, the existence of "reprobate infants."

CALVIN.[5]—"If *those*, therefore, *to whom the Lord hath vouchsafed His election,* having received the sign of regeneration, *depart this life before they grow up,* He reneweth them by the power of His Spirit."

MUSCULUS.[6] —"Since, therefore, this discrimination of *elect* and *reprobate*, in *newborn infants (recens natis infantibus)*, is hidden from our judgment, it is not fitting that we should inquire into it, lest by ignorance we reject vessels of grace."

---

[3] Of the Efficacy of Baptism in Infants. Mis. Sacr., II. 621.
[4] XXVIII. VI.
[5] Institutes, IV., XVI., 21.
[6] Loci Communes, 336.

MARTYR.[7]—"What is to be judged of the soul of a child so killed, having as yet not received the sacrament (of circumcision)? I answer that we, either as touching his salvation or condemnation, can affirm nothing on either side. For if he pertained to the number of the elect so that he was predestinate to eternal life, there is no cause but that he may be saved. But if he were a vessel to *that end made* of God, *to show forth in him His wrath*, and so *to be condemned*, what can we complain of the severity of God, especially seeing we are all born the children of wrath and of condemnation?"

ALSTED John Henry (1588-1638) says of Baptism.— "The children of unbelievers are not to be baptized—the children, both of whose parents are believers or one of whom is a believer, are to be baptized—for the infants of believers are in the covenant. If the covenant, which is the greater thing, belongs to them, much more does the seal, which is the less. The faith of parents benefits infants."[8] "The mode of federation, with respect to infants (we mean the infants of believers, who die before they reach the years of discretion) is almost hidden to us. Yet this is certain, that in the foundation of the covenant of grace, they are justified, and blessed, and hence are endowed with true faith. *Elect* infants are falsely called unbelievers, for though elect infants who die in infancy, for of these we speak, be destitute of what is called actual faith, they are not on that account destitute of all faith. For as they have the Holy Spirit, it is impossible that there should be no operation of the Holy Spirit in them; though it be secret and unknown to us. Nor can they be called unbelievers. For as Christ is received by faith only, and

[7] Common Places, IV. 110.
[8] Theologia, Scholastica Didictica, Hanoviæ. 1618, 4to. pp. 815, 816. The copy we use is in the library of the University of Pennsylvania.

Christ is given to elect infants, as having union and communion with Him; we cannot deny that they have faith. Faith in principle and seed, and virtually, is to be attributed to elect infants."[9]

The Swiss THEOLOGIANS at Dort[10] say: "That there is an *election and reprobation of infants, no less than of adults,* we cannot deny, in the face of *God* who loves,* and *hates, unborn children* (*nondum natos amat, et odit*)."

CHAMIER.[11]—"In the case of these (*infants*) Paul has most expressly established by testimonies of Scripture, that there is not only a *predestination* unto *salvation,* but also a *reprobation.* And indeed it must *either* be asserted *that no infants* are destined to punishment, *or* it must be confessed that some are destined without respect to co-operation or repugnance. Since the *former is absurd,* the second is to be held as true." "There are two classes of mankind who perish, some utterly deserted in natural corruption, and ignorance of Divine Truth, as the *most part of infants* outside the Church."[12]

MARK FREDERIC WENDELIN (1584—1652) was one of the greatest of the German Reformed dogmaticians, and polemics of the Seventeenth Century. His Theologia Christiana (the smaller work—the larger one was posthumous 1656) first appeared 1634, and was reviewed by John Gerhard, to whom Wendelin refers in his Theological Exercitations, 1652. In this very elaborate defense of Calvinism, he shows at large, that

"Baptism does not change infants spiritually," "that none are to be admitted to Baptism, but those who are in God's covenant," and the "arguments are answered by which Lutherans prove that all infants are

---

[9] Do. 785.
[10] Acta Synod. Dordr. Judie. 40.
[11] Panstrat. Cathol. III., viii., 8,. 11,14,117.
[12] Panstrat. Cathol . VII., i., 18, 99.

regenerated in the Act of Baptism.[13] "That Baptism, as a laver of regeneration, is applied for the remission of sins, all the Reformed Churches teach. But it is one thing to say, that infants are baptized for the remission of sins, it is another thing to say, that they are baptized, that they may be regenerated."[14] Gerhard had urged that if "the hypothesis of the absolute decree of reprobation stands, this affirmation can be made, not of all infants, but of the *elect* only, as in truth, the Calvinistic doctors in various passages, actually explain it." Wendelin with perfect frankness replies: "There is no need here of inferences or of citations, to convince me. Of my own accord, and freely and expressly I confess, with *Ursinus* and our other teachers, that not all who are baptized, whether adults or *infants*, become participants of the grace of Christ, for the election of God is most free: it is therefore a *prerogative of the elect alone*, which Baptism seals."[15]

"With one mouth, all the Reformed Churches teach that all the infants of Christians, draw from their nativity original sin, and through it are obnoxious to eternal death." "*All infants* of Christians, even before Baptism are holy, with a federal and external holiness, on account of which they ought to be reputed a part of the visible Church and people of God, and as federates be admitted to the seal of the covenant. *Some infants* of Christians, even before Baptism, nay even in their mothers' womb, not indeed by nature, but by grace, are holy with an internal sanctity, and *these infants are believers and regenerate. Charity presumes* this sanctity in regard to each one, no less before Baptism, than after it." "The internal sanctity is not necessarily conjoined with the federal, but in *many infants* and adults is

---

[13] Exercitationes Theologicte, Casselis. 1652,4to. See the very copious Index: Baptismus.
[14] Exercitatio. xxxvii. §18.
[15] Exercitatio. xxxvii. 19.

separated from it. This we learn from the event; for those who were once sanctified never wholly lose their sanctity."[16] "The case of infants born of those not federate is different, to whom that grace is not promised. Hence they are not federate, and, still less regenerated by the Spirit."[17] "In general it is very truly said, of a Christian is born, not a heathen but a Christian, as a Jew is born of a Jew, a citizen of a citizen."[18] "The Word of God has no efficacy unless it be understood. The Spirit of God operates without the word, not only on infants born, but on infants unborn."[19]

WESTMINSTER CONFESSION X. iii.— "Elect infants, dying in infancy, are regenerated."

§ 7. INFANTS WORTHY OF PERDITION.

For Calvinism holds that all infants are bound over to God's wrath and made subject to eternal misery; that is, that God might justly condemn forever every infant.

HEIDEGGER:[20] (1633—1698) — "For original sin the penalty is eternal; it is the penalty both of loss and of sense, the sense both of the worm, and of the fire, though in some, as for example *in infants* it is milder, in others it is severer."

WESTMINSTER CONFESSION. XI., vi.— "*Every* sin both *original* and actual, * * * doth, in its own nature, bring guilt upon the sinner, whereby he is bound over to the wrath of God and curse of the law, and so made subject to death, with all miseries, spiritual, temporal,

---

[16] Exercitatio. xxxvii. 1.
[17] Do. 15.
[18] Do 3.
[19] Do. 8.
[20] Do. 10.

and *eternal.*"[21]

§ 8. ACTUAL PERDITION OF INFANTS ACCORDING TO CALVINISM.

Holding that all infants deserve damnation, that the election of God alone can save them from it, and that this election does not extend to all infants, Calvinism of necessity teaches that some infants perish.

CALVIN.[22] — "As to infants they seem to perish not by their own fault but by the fault of another; but there is a double solution. Though sin does not yet appear in them, yet it is latent; for they bear corruption shut up in the soul, so that before God they are damnable."

"That infants who are to be saved (as certainly out of that age *some* are saved) must be before regenerated by the Lord is clear."[23]

Holding that infants must be regenerated in order to be saved, Calvinism teaches that some infants die *unregenerated,* and are lost.

MARTYR.[24] — "Augustine adjudgeth young infants to hell fire, if they die *not regenerated.* And the Holy Scriptures do seem to favor his part; for in the last judgment, there shall be but only a double sentence pronounced. There is no third place appointed between the saved and condemned * * * We will say, therefore, with Augustine, and with the Holy Scripture, that they *must be punished.*"

SPANHEIM, the elder, in arguing against the universality of the Divine will, that men should be saved, says: "Either God wills to have mercy unto the salvation of the Gentiles outside of the covenant,

---

[21] Corpus Theologiæ, Tigur, 1700. Fol. I. 361.
[22] Ezekiel XVIII., Opera iv. 167.
[23] Institut. iv. xvi. 17.
[24] Common Place, I., 234.

whether deprived of *life in the cradle*, in the *earliest infancy*, or attaining to some age, or He does not If He does not, the universality of His pity goes to the ground. If He does, it follows that to numberless ones to whom not a word concerning Christ and the Gospel was ever made known, *there exists a way to salvation, outside of Christ and the covenant of God.*" "The universal pity overthrows the decree of election and reprobation.[25]"

MOLINAEUS. [26] — "Of the infants of unbelievers." "We dare not promise salvation to any (infant) remaining outside Christ's covenant. They are indeed by nature 'children of wrath' (Eph. ii. 3), and 'strangers from the covenant of promise,' ([[Verse 12 >> Eph 2.12]]). They are pronounced (1 Corinth, vii. 14) 'unclean,' while that they are contrasted with the 'holy.' From which curse, inasmuch as no one is freed except through Christ, I do not find that the benefit of Christ pertains to them."

COCCEIUS. [27] — "Elect Infants" * * "are not conceived and born as are the children of the Gentiles, concerning whom the *presumption is certain*, that they, with their mother's milk, drink in godlessness unto destruction."

DR. TWISS, *Prolocutor of the Westminster Assembly.* — WILLIAM TWISS (1575—1646) was renowned for his learning, his piety, and his rigid Calvinism. He was a strong Supralapsarian. He nobly represents the firmness and internal consistency of the true old Calvinist. He was worthy the honor conferred on him by both Houses of Parliament, in electing him Prolocutor of the Westminster Assembly of Divines. "He was universally allowed to be the ablest opponent

---

[25] Exercitat. de Grat., universali, 4.
[26] Thesaurus Disputit. Theolog. in Sedan. Acad. Genev. 1661. I. 212.
[27] Cateches. Palat. Quaes LXXIV.

of Arminianism in that age." His greatest work is his Vindicise Gratiae,[28] his Vindication of the Grace, Power and Providence of God. It was written in reply to the Criticism of Arrninius (1560— 1609) on Perkins, (1558—1602).

Twiss says: "*Many* Infants depart from this life in original sin, and consequently are condemned to eternal death, on account of original sin alone: therefore from the sole transgression of Adam condemnation to eternal death has *followed upon many infants.*"[29]

(WESTMINSTER CONFESSION: X., iii., iv.: "*Elect infants* * * are saved. * * So too are all other elect persons. Others not elected * * cannot be saved."

The doctrine of genuine Calvinism then is that there are reprobate infants who are left to the total penalty which original sin brings and merits.

What that is, the Larger Catechism defines: "The fall brought upon mankind the loss of communion with God, his displeasure and curse; so that we are by nature children of wrath, bound slaves to Satan, and justly liable to all punishments in this world and that which is to come.' The punishments of sin in the world to come "are everlasting separation from the comfortable presence of God, and most grievous torments in soul and body, without intermission, in hell-fire forever." (Q. 29) In this state of sin and misery God *leaves* all men, except his elect. (Q. 30). "*Every sin,* both *original* and actual, * * * doth in its own nature bring guilt upon the sinner, whereby he is bound over to the wrath of God and curse of the law, and so made subject to death, with ALL the miseries, spiritual, temporal, and ETERNAL." (Westminster Confess. VI., 6).

---

[28] The first Edition was published 1632, Folio. The one from which we quote is the Second. Amsterdam, 1632. 4to. It is in the Library of the University of Pennsylvania.

[29] Vindiciae, I. 48.

It is from this the "elect infants" are delivered, it 8 to this the "reprobate infants" are abandoned.

§ 9. PRESUMPTION AND ASSURANCE IN REGARD TO INFANTS.

Calvinism has the "certain presumption" that the children of unbelievers are lost, but Calvinism has no assurance that the infants of believers are saved.

MARTYR[30]— Neither must it be thought that I would promise salvation unto all the children of the faithful, which depart without the sacrament (baptism): for if I should do so I might be counted rash. I leave them to be judged of the mercy of God, seeing I have no knowledge of the secret election and predestination. "I *dare not promise* certain salvation, particularly unto *any* that departeth hence. For there be some children of the saints which belong not unto predestination."[31]

"The children of the godly, departing without baptism, *may* be saved * * * *if* they appertain to the number of such as be predestinate. Also, I do except all others, *if any there be*, which by the secret council of God belong unto perdition."[32]

CHAMIER.[33]— "We deny that sins are really forgiven them who do not belong to the eternal election: as Esau was never forgiven, *though he was circumcised*, for he was hateful to God before he was born."

MASSON (BECMAN.) [34] — "*Not all baptized* children are true regenerate Christians, who shall be saved; for God the Lord hath reserved to Himself His

---

[30] Common Places. Trans, by Marten, 1533. IV., 120.
[31] Common Places., I., 233.
[32] Common Places, IV., 187. He uses nearly the same words in his Comm. on Rom. V., 304.
[33] L., XIII., de Fid. Cap. XXI., 34, p. 224.
[34] VI., 90.

secret foreknowledge toward children, also, yet *unborn."*

PAREUS.[35] — "Neither Zwingli, nor Calvin, nor any one of us, places, without distinction in heaven with the saints, *all infants who die without baptism, whether unborn or in birth, or while they are carried to baptism,* but they pronounce this, by the law of charity, of the infants alone of the Church, born in the covenant if they be prevented by death * * * nevertheless, without *interference with the election* of God, which as of old in the family of Abraham and Isaac, so in after time *often hath made, and doth make a discrimination between* the *children of* believers, a discrimination which we are neither to search into nor to scoff at, but to adore. (Rom. ix. 11). This is the constant judgment of ourselves, and of our divines concerning this question."

BODIUS.[36] — "Nor yet, meanwhile, do we so bind to the faith of believing parents the grace and pity of God toward infants, as to do any prejudice to His free and *secret* election; who knoweth *His own,* whether of *infants* or adult professors of faith, and hath them sealed with a seal *known to Himself alone."*

WITSIUS.[37] — "These (the prerogatives of the federated infants) are not to be stretched to the point of supposing that *all the children* of pious parents are *ordained* to salvation. For Holy Scripture and daily experience prove that the offspring of the best, mature into the very worst condition of soul, and are persistent to their own destruction."

Hence a doubt that the parent was elect, cast doubt on the presumption that the infant was elect, and the overthrow of the proof that the parent was elect destroyed the presumption that the child was elect.

---

[35] Castigat. in. Bellarmin. de amissione gratiae. 1613. L.VI., 871.
[36] On Ephes. quoted by Witsius. Misc. Sacr. II., 617.
[37] Miscel. Sacr. II., 615.

SIBEL.— [38] "We admonish parents that they should enter into themselves, and should search themselves whether they are partakers of the covenant, endowed with saving faith, armed with the purpose of new obedience. *If they discern this in themselves*, there is no reason why they should doubt of the election and salvation of the children whom God has called out of this life in infancy."

§ 10. The Election of Children and their Death.

Calvinism cannot consistently allow that the infantile age, or the time of the child's death, is in any way connected with the moral probabilities of its election.

THE THEOLOGIANS OF GREAT BRITAIN, at the Synod of Dort, argue against the Remonstrant proposition that "all infants dying before the use of reason are saved," the Arminian position then, the Calvinistic opinion according to Dr. Hodge now. In their argument they declare as their official judgment:[39] "As regards the Divine election, the circumstance of *age* is a thing *that does not belong thereto* (*impertinens*), and has no effect whatever, (*nihil prorsus operatur.*")

WESTMINSTER CONFESSION, Chap. III., v. —"Those of mankind that are predestinated unto life, God, * * according to the *secret* counsel * * of His will * * hath chosen * * out of His mere free grace and love, without any foresight of faith * * *or any other thing* in the creature, as conditions or causes moving Him thereunto."

Either the foreseen something in the creature, to wit, its early death, moves God, or it does not. If it moves Him, the doctrine of absolute predestination is annihilated; if it does not move Him, the whole moral

---

[38] In Ep. Jud., Vol. IV., 138.
[39] Acta Synod. Dordrechti habit. Dordr. 1620. Judic, p. 10.

presumption in regard to any difference in favor of dying infants is of no force whatever. And yet it is obviously this moral presumption which has overcome the stern demands of the system, has made Calvinists deny what even Arminians under the stress created by Calvinism were at first compelled to admit, and has led them not only to reject the doctrine of infant damnation, but has made them unwilling to believe that it was ever implied in their Confession, and maintained by their divines. Nor have there been wanting Calvinistic divines of the highest order, who have abandoned entirely this part of the Calvinistic doctrine, and have accepted in substance the Lutheran view. Such were Le Blanc, and Jurieu.[40] Nor can we wonder at this. The Calvinistic system furnishes no ground of *positive assurance* that any infant whatever dying in infancy is saved. As Lutherans, we have a clear faith resting on a specific covenant in the case of a baptized child, and a well-grounded hope resting on an all-embracing mercy in the case of an unbaptized child.

To Calvinism the baptism authenticates nothing. What it is in any case, even as a sign, is a secret bound up with another secret. The most that Calvinism can do in the most hopeful case is to cherish a *presumption* in charity, that the child's parents may be elect, and a presumption on that presumption that the child may be elect, and therefore saved— while in the darkest case the presumption is that the class of children it embraces is lost. The same element in Calvinism, which on the basis of a *secret* council forbids it to affirm of any one particular child that that child is lost, forbids it equally to affirm of any one particular child that that child is certainly saved: and the sort of presumption on which Calvinism argues that a few children *may* be saved, is overwhelming in fixing the

[40] Witsius, Miscell. Sacr. II. Exc. XIX. LXII. LXIV.

conclusion that the great masses of children are lost.

§ 11. HEREDITARY RIGHTS OF INFANTS.

Calvinism holds that the rights of infants in the Church are *hereditary* rights, bound up with their natural descent.

CALVIN.[41] — "Unless God transmit His grace from the fathers to the sons, to receive new-born infants into the Church, would be a mere profanation of Baptism." "The children of *believers*, who are horn in the Church, we say are of the household of the kingdom of God. * * Inasmuch as God hath adopted the children of believers, before they were born, we draw the inference that they are not to be defrauded of the outward sign."[42]

ZANCHIUS.[43] — "All are to be baptized who, on account of the piety of the parents are believed to belong to the covenant."

WITSIUS.[44]— "It is a thing confessed by all the orthodox (the Calvin* ists), that, although it be not safe curiously to search into the secrets of the divine counsels, and to determine many things concerning the lot of infants, dying in infancy; yet that the *prerogative* is great, of those infants, whose *parents* are in the *saving communion* of God's covenant."

WESTMINSTER CONFESSION, xxvii.: "The visible Church ... consists of all those throughout the world that profess the true religion, *together with their children.*" So Larger Catechism, Q. 62.

---

[41] II. Defens. de Sacrament. Opera VIII. 683.
[42] On Acts X. 47.
[43] Opera, VIII. 516.
[44] De Efficac. Bapt. in Infantib. Miscell. Sacr. II. 615.

§ 12. HEREDITARY EXEMPTION FROM THE COMMON LOT.

Hence in the Calvinistic system the children of believers seem to be exempt from the common lot in some sense.

CALVIN. [45] —The propagation of sin and damnation in the seed of Adam is universal; all, therefore, not one excepted, are included within this curse, whether they spring from believers or from the godless... The condition of nature is therefore equal in all, so that they are subject alike to sin and eternal death. That the Apostle here attributes a *special* privilege to the children of believers, flows from the blessing of the covenant, by the supervention of which the curse of nature is removed. The *children of believers* are exempted from the *common lot of the human* race, as they are separated unto the Lord." "Those that were without (the church), were not to be admitted to baptism till they had made a profession of faith. But the *infant children of believers*, as they were adopted from the womb, and by right of the promise, pertained to the body of the Church, were baptized."

§ 13. JUDAIZING VIEW.

The logical Calvinism runs out in fact into a *Judaizing* construction of the covenant, and of the relation of infants to it.

PAREUS.[46] — "The children of Christians are born Christians, as the children of Jews were born Jews." "They are born in the covenant and are citizens of the Church." "The infants of Christians are citizens of the Church, are born in the covenant, with federal grace, and saints of saints: as citizens are born of citizens, the free are born of the free, slaves are born of

---

[45] 1 Corinth. vii. 14. Hebrews vi. 2.
[46] Irenicon, 262.

slaves."[47]

GURTLER.[48] — "Christian infants are federates of God, partakers of the good things promised in the covenant, citizens of the kingdom of heaven, defended by angels, and heirs of eternal life, *therefore* not to be deprived of the sign of the covenant."

All this they are (if elect) born to in their natural birth of believers, and having all this already, the sign is to be given them.

§ 14. CUTTING OFF OF INFANTS FROM THE COVENANT.

The Calvinistic system holds that the parental neglect to have a child baptized cuts off the child from the covenant, as in the Jewish nation.

CALVIN.[49] — "Inasmuch as it is not in man's good pleasure to sunder what God has joined together: no one can spurn or neglect the sign, without casting away the Word itself, and depriving himself of the blessing therein offered. Whosoever, Baptism neglected, pretends that he is content with the bare promise, treads under foot, as far as in him lies, the blood of Christ, or at least *permits it not to flow to his children*, who are to be washed. Therefore *the contempt* of the sign is followed by the just penalty, *the privation of grace*, inasmuch as by the godless divorce, or rather the tearing asunder of the sign and of the Word, the covenant of God is violated."

COCCEIUS.—[50] "If they be not baptized, there would be an *abnegation of the covenant of God*, as if believers had not a promise concerning their children, but as if they were in the same lot in which the children

---

[47] Comm. in Rom. XI. 1143.
[48] Instit. Theolog. 844.
[49] On Genes. XVII. 14. Opera, Amstelod. 1671, p. 91.
[50] Catechesis. Rel. Christ. Q. LXIV.

of unbelievers are."

§ 15. ELECT PARENTS AND ELECT INFANTS.

The *presumption* that infants are *elect* is based upon the *presumption* that the parents are *elect*. It is not enough that the parents are members of the visible Church, nor that before men they sustain a good character for piety—they must be elect.

GOMARUS.[51]— "We piously believe that the *infants* of *those who are in God's covenant through Christ, and true believers*, are also elect."

In the various passages we have cited, it is always the presumption that the parents are elect and therefore believers; that is the basis of the presumption that their children are elect. The Church membership of the parent, in itself has no bearing on the election of the child, except that when people profess religion, we charitably presume they have it, and presuming that they are elect, we presume that their children may be elect.

§ 16. A PIOUS FICTION.

But this presumption is but a presumption in any case. In the best case the faith of elect parents that their children are certainly sanctified, rests after all on a *pious fiction*. No parent can, according to logical Calvinism, have any real assurance in regard to any particular child, that it is elect, sanctified, and in the covenant.

BEZA, at the Colloquy at MONTBELIARD:[52] "The Holy Spirit exercises His power in the elect alone... the others who are condemned, and not elect, being left...

---

[51] Acta Synod, Dord. III. 24.

[52] Acta Colloq. Montis Belligartensis. Anno C. 1586. Tubingae, 1594. p. 479. Do-auz dein Latein verteutscht: Tubingen, 1587, p. 837.

The adoption is *offered* in circumcision, to all who are circumcised; but the *elect* alone receive it, whose eyes God has opened, that they may see and be saved. The rest, to whom God hath not vouchsafed this grace, are left to His righteous judgment, and yet God remains true. The same takes place in Baptism, which *many thousand infants receive*, who yet are never regenerated, but *perish forever.*"

Beza's words, as they were generally understood, were so often quoted against the Calvinistic system, that Christian Becmann (under the assumed name of Masson) insists that they have been perverted, and that Beza meant that "many thousands of baptized children become godless and are lost, after they reach the age of adults." Masson could hardly have read the Acts of the Colloquy, or he would have seen that in Andreæ's reply to Beza, are these words: "It is a very dreadful thing to hear you say that many thousand infants are baptized, who are never regenerated, but perish forever; nor do I think there is a single person in this body of hearers who will agree with you in this." To this Beza replied not a word. Andreæ further said: "It is a bad thing on your part that you leave pious parents in perpetual doubt whether their children have been adopted as sons of God through the Baptism they have received. For according to your answers... it cannot and ought not to be certainly pronounced that a baptized infant is adopted as God's child or regenerated, but that it should only be *thought probable* that they will be endowed with the fruit of adoption, God's secret judgment being left to Himself."

To this Beza replied: "Each of us can judge and pronounce concerning ourselves, whether we be regenerate or not; but a judgment concerning others may be doubtful and false."

MOMMA, [53] who boasts that it was his "supremest solicitude not to depart a nails breadth from the faith and Confession of the Reformed Church," is more candid than Masson, and stamps Andreæ with the epithet "crude," for his counter judgment to Beza.

BEZA.[54] – "If it be objected that not *all born* of faithful parents are elect, and consequently not all sanctified, since God did not elect all the children of Abraham and Isaac, we are not without an answer. *For though we do not in the least deny that these things are so*; yet we say this secret judgment is to be left to God, and *in general* (unless there be something in the way, from which the opposite can be gathered), we presume from the formula of promise, that they who are born of faithful parents, or of one faithful parent, are sanctified."

ZANCHIUS:[55] "We believe that elect infants, when they are baptized, are not baptized with water alone, but are endowed also with the Spirit of Regeneration."

BUCAN.[56]— "Children (born of believing parents, or of one believing parent,) the Apostle calls 'holy' (1 Cor. vii. 14): that is pure and separated to the Lord. * Nor is it in the way of this, *that not all born of faithful parents are elect*, for it is not for us to search into the secret judgments of God; but we with good reason suppose all born of Christians *probably* elect."

GUERTLER.[57] — "Many sprinkled with water both *infants* and adults, do not obtain salvation, beyond doubt because they do not receive *Baptism entire*, but only its first and most common part."

---

[53] De Varia Conditione, sub Occonom., etc. Basilese 1718, II.207.
[54] De Spirit. Sac. IV. 29.
[55] Opera, VII. 48.
[56] Institut. Theolog. Loc. XLVII. 29.
[57] Institut. Theolog. Amstelod. 1694. Ch. XXXIII. 178.

WITSIUS.[58]— "Baptism does not signify nor seal, still less does it confer on *all* infants of those who are in the covenant, any common justification, regeneration and sanctification. * * or remission of original sin, either a revocable or irrevocable remission. But all efficacy of Baptism, which involves a state of salvation, even in respect of *their age*, is confined to *elect infants* alone (*solis electis infantibus proprium*)."

LEYDECKER.[59]— "The faith demanded of parents in the formula of Baptism is *indefinite*: This, to wit that godly persons' infants are *sanctified* in Christ. And that faith is true, although there should be here and there *an exception...* That divine promise has a *common* truth, though God *reserve to Himself*, according to His own power and liberty, *the exclusion of some infants*. Faith ... performs its office when it lays hold of the promise as it is given, and reverently leaves to God *liberty of application*. The believer is bound ... to acquiesce in the promise given ... and to trust in it, or, in the judgment of charity to hope well concerning this infant which is to be baptized—nay, to believe that *this* infant belongs to Christ, *unless* God, by a singular decision, *wills its* exclusion. The faith demanded of parents is not vain... though *here and there one* (of the infants) *does not belong to the election*...although there is not an internal baptizing of exactly all infants."

WESTMINSTER CONFESSION X. M. IV. "*Elect* infants dying in infancy are regenerated. So, also, are *all other elect* persons. Others not elected ... cannot be saved."

§ 17. RESERVE.

Hence logical Calvinism speaks with *reserve*

---

[58] De Effic. Baptism, Misc-Sac. II. 622.
[59] De Veritat. Fid. Ref. siv. Comm. in Catech. Palat. Ultraj. 1694, p. 327

even of the cases of infants, which are most hopeful. "If the infants of *believers* die in infancy before the years of discretion, we have good *hopes* concerning them," say the Swiss theologians at Dort.[60] "By the law of *charity*" says Pareus,[61] and so through the whole. Millions of the children of pagans and of other reprobates are certainly lost, and some, *if* their parents be elect, *may* be saved. We reach again the point to which we came before. Calvinism has no ground on which it can affirm positively and unerringly, on *its own premises*, that any one particular child dying in infancy is certainly saved. In place of a distinct Christian assurance based on a positive covenant, it has assumption based on assumption, presumption built on presumption, hopes resting on hopes, Charity confessing that ignorance of a terrible secret is its mother. The worst position in which a brighter faith can suppose a child to be, is the best which Calvinism can assign it.

§18. BAPTISM AND ANABAPTISM.

CALVINISM rests the validity of Baptism not on what it brings, but on what it finds:

LATTER CONFESSION OF HELVETIA. (1566)—Why should not they be consecrated by holy Baptism, who are God's peculiar people, and in the Church of God?[62]

MOLINAEUS.[63] — "The Baptism of water is not, therefore, absolutely necessary to the reconciliation of the infant and its reception into grace: inasmuch as the *reconciliation precedes* the Baptism."

---

[60] Judicta. 40.

[61] Castigat. in quatuor Lib. Bellam. de amisione gratiae et. Statu Peccat. Heidelberg, 1613. L. vi. 891.

[62] Ch. xx. Ed. Augusti, 72. Nemeyer, 518. Beck. I. 158. Hall's Harm. of Conf. 302.

[63] Quoted by Witsius, M. S. II. 627.

VOETIUS.[64] — "The opinion of the Reformed theologians is known, that the efficacy of Baptism is not in *producing* regeneration, but in sealing regeneration *already* produced."

WITSIUS [65] — "God is not only free to confer the grace of regeneration on *elect infants before* the use of *Baptism*, but it is credible that He *ordinarily does so.*" The margin applies this "to those who die in infancy," but the text shows conclusively that Witsius does not limit the principle to them.

THE LITURGY OF THE CHURCH OF HOLLAND required parents, presenting their children for Baptism, to confess that they "acknowledged them as *sanctified* in *Christ*, and, on *that account, as members* of His Church, to be Baptized."

§19. GRACE BEFORE BAPTISM.

Grace in no sense waits on Baptism, but Baptism waits on Grace: Baptism is not a means of Grace, but Grace is a means of real Baptism; in the Calvinistic System we are baptized not in order to obtain Grace, but because we are supposed already to have it.

CALVIN. — "They are embraced in the covenant *from the womb.*" "By what right could we admit them to Baptism, except that they are heirs of the promise? For unless already *before it* (*jam ante*) the promise of life pertained to them, he would profane Baptism who would give it to them."

MARTYR.[66] — "Little ones, who truly belong to this election, are endowed with the Holy Spirit *before* they are baptized." "Nor would we baptize little children, unless we supposed that they *already* belong

---

[64] Quoted by Witsius. M. S. II. 633.
[65] Misc. Sac. II. 631.
[66] Loc. Com. IV. viii.

to the Church and to Christ."

FORMER CONFESSION OF HELVETIA (1530-32).—
"Baptism is the font of regeneration, the which the Lord
doth give to *his elect* (*electis suis*). In which holy font we
baptize our infants. Especially seeing that we ought
godly to *presume* of their election."[67]

RIVETUS.[68] — "True Baptism requires that they
shall be in the covenant, to whom it is administered."

AMES.[69] — "Unless they are to be esteemed as
members of the Church, they ought not to be baptized.
For Baptism is, in its own nature, the seal of an
ingrafting *already made* into Christ, and, consequently,
into His Church."

§20. BAPTISM WITHOUT OBJECTIVE FORCE.

According to Calvinism, Baptism has no
objective force even to elect infants.

ZURICH CONSENSUS,[70] between Calvin and the
Zurich ministers 1549: "Whatever good is conferred on
us by (the Sacraments) is not by their own virtue, even
though you comprehend in it the promises. The
Sacraments are *called* seals, but the Spirit alone is
properly the seal."

HEIDELBERG CATECHISM.[71] — "Is the outward
Baptism of water that washing away of sin? It is not,
for the blood of Christ (and the Holy Spirit) alone,
purges us from all sin."

BODIUS,[72] arguing against the view that
children are not members of Christ *before* Baptism,

---

[67] 15 in Rom. VI.
[68] Art. xxi. Ed. Augusti, 99, Ed. Niemeyer, 112, 120. Beck, I.
55. Hall's Harmony, 303.
[69] Ad Genes. Exerc. 88, p. 429.
[70] Enerv. Bellarm. II. 49.
[71] Niemeyer, Coll. Conf.
[72] Qu. LXXII. Augusti, 556. Niemeyer, 408, 445.

says: "If this opinion were true, it would follow that the children of Christians, no less than of Turks, Jews, and heathen, should be prohibited from Baptism until they are of a fitting age to make a profession of faith for themselves; for there is no reason why the seal of the covenant should be impressed on those who have nothing to do with the covenant itself."

WITSIUS.[73]— "Communion with Christ, and with His mystic body seems to *precede* Baptism in elect infants; at least in the judgment of charity. For as an argument for infant Baptism, the orthodox (Calvinists) constantly say: They to whom belong the covenant of grace, the fellowship of Christ and of the Church, and whose is the kingdom of heaven, ought to be baptized. But all these things belong to *elect and* federate infants."

§21. DEFINITION OF BAPTISM.

Dr. Heppe, in his Dogmatic of the Evangelical Reformed Church, (1861), presents the doctrines of the Calvinistic Churches, and illustrates his text with citations from their *standard theologians.*

THE definitions of Baptism which Heppe gives as purely Calvinistic and Reformed, are as follows: "Baptism is a sacrament, in which those *to whom the covenant of God's grace pertains,* are washed with water in the name of the Father, Son, and Holy Spirit, that is, that to those who are baptized, it is *signified and sealed,* that they are received into the *communion* of the covenant of grace, *are inserted into Christ,* and His mystic body, the Church, are justified by God, for the sake of Christ's blood shed for us, and *regenerated* by Christ's Spirit." This definition he gives from POLANUS. Another and shorter one he furnishes from WOLLEBIUS as follows: "Baptism is the first sacrament of the new covenant, in which to the *elect* received into the family

---

[73] Quoted by Witsius, 191.

of God, by the outward application of water, *the remission of sins and regeneration by the blood of Christ and by the Holy Spirit are sealed.*" He gives only one other, which is from HEIDEGGER, thus: Baptism is the *sacrament of regeneration, in which to each and to every one embraced in the covenant of God, the inward washing from sins through the blood and Spirit of Christ,* is declared *and sealed.*

§ 22. BAPTISM OF NON-ELECT INFANTS.

Calvinism particularly gives prominence to the idea that non-elect infants receiving Baptism, receive no benefit.

ZURICH CONSENSUS, between Calvin and the Zurich ministers.— "We zealously teach that God does not promiscuously exercise His power on all who receive the Sacraments, but only on the elect. He enlightens unto faith none but those whom *He has foreordained unto life.* By the *secret power* (arcana virtute) of His Spirit, he effects that *the elect* receive those things which the sacraments offer."[74] "To the *reprobate* equally with the *elect* the signs are administered, but the truth of the signs reaches only the *latter.*"[75]

ZANCHIUS.[76] — "The power of Baptism has place in the elect alone. They only are baptized, not with water merely but with the Spirit also. Though all these things (enumerated previously) are affirmed of Baptism, and are truly attributed to it as the organ of the Holy Spirit, and all who are baptized are truly said to become and be such *Sacramentally*; yet we believe that these things are fulfilled *in fact*, only in the elect. All are baptized with water, but the elect only, with the

---

[74] De Efficac. Baptis. in Inf. Misc. Sac. II. 725.
[75] Niemeyer, Collect. Conf. 195.
[76] Opera, VIII. 516.

Spirit; all receive the sign, but the *elect only* are made partakers of the thing signified and offered through Baptism."

BUCAN.[77]— "Incorporation into Christ, and the benefits which follow it, are in no wise really conferred on the reprobate, though he be baptized with water. For God efficaciously calls, justifies, regenerates, and glorifies those only whom He has *chosen* and *predestinated* to these things. The *elect*, whether *infants* or adults, whether in Baptism or before Baptism, are equally incorporated in Christ."

Witsius[78]— "On such Baptism confers *nothing* truly good; it signifies or seals *no* grace, *no* salvation; no more than a piece of wax, with a beautiful stamp on it, attached to a blank sheet of paper—or, if you prefer, attached to a sheet so defiled with blots that nothing good can be written on it. Well has Robert, Bishop of Salisbury, said: 'Sacraments, as they are seals of grace, and of God's promise, exert their power spiritually in *those only* who are sons of the promise and heirs of grace.'"

§ 23. INFANTS OUTSIDE OF THE CHURCH.

Calvinism therefore holds, that as infants who are born of parents who are outside of the Church, are not of the Church, they are not to be baptized.

BUCAN.[79] — "Infants descended from believing and baptized parents are to be baptized—but the children of unbelievers, who are not in the Church, and the children of the unbaptized, are *not* to be baptized." "Are not the little ones of the unbelievers, neglected by them, and taken into the care of Christians, to be baptized? No, not till they become adults ..."

---

[77] Institutiones Theol. Genev. 1625. Loc. XLVII. p. 54.
[78] Miscell. Sacr. II. 618.
[79] Institutiones Theologicae. Genev. 1625, 624.

WESTMINSTER CONFESSION, XXVIII. iv. — "The infants of ONE or BOTH *believing parents* are to be baptized."

LARGER CATECHISM. (Qu. 166).— "Baptism is *not* to be administered to *any that are out of the visible Church* ... but infants descended from parents, either, both, or but one of them professing faith in Christ, and obedience to Him, are ... to be baptized."

§ 24. CALVINISM AND ANABAPTISM.

Hence Calvinism narrows to the last degree any real difference between its own views and those of *Anabaptists*, or Baptists. In stating the points of controversy between Calvinists and Mennonites and other *Anabaptists*, the Calvinist divines constantly represent themselves and the *Anabaptists* as perfectly agreed, so far as the Baptism of the children of unbelievers is concerned.

The Calvinistic argument against the *Anabaptist* objection to infant Baptism, constantly rests on the theory, that infants have a right to Baptism only as they possess certain spiritual qualifications. Where those qualifications are not to be presumed the Anabaptist objection stands, and Calvinism concedes it.

Thus BULLINGER.[80]—"The kingdom of heaven is of infants. No man is received into the kingdom of heaven unless he be the friend of God: and these are not destitute of the Spirit of God. Children are God's, therefore they have the Spirit of God. Therefore, if they have received the Holy Spirit as well as we; if they he accounted among the people of God as well as we that be grown of age, who can forbid these to be baptized with water in the name of the Lord?"

VAN HOEKE.[81] — "There is no question between

---

[80] Sermons on the Sacraments Cambridge, 1840, 183.
[81] Lucubrationes in Cateches. Palat. Lugduni 1711, p. 310.

us and the Mennonites as to whether the infants of unbelievers, or of those who are outside of the covenant of God, are to be baptized? For *to these*, both WE and THEY deny Baptism. But the question is, whether the infants of those *who are in the* covenant, or *one* of whose parents is in the covenant, are to be baptized?"

THE CONFESSION OF SCOTLAND (1560).— "Baptism appertaineth to the infants *of the faithful.* And so we condemn the error of the Anabaptists."[82]

THE LATTER HELVETIC CONFESSION (Chap. xx). — "We condemn the Anabaptists who deny that the *new-born children of the faithful* are to be baptized. For of *these* ... is the kingdom of God, and they are in the covenant of God. Why, therefore, should not the sign of God's covenant be given *them?* Why shall not they be initiated by holy Baptism, who are *God's own*, and in the Church of God?"[83]

CONFESSION OF FRANCE (1559).— "Seeing that together with the parents, God doth account their posterity also to be *of the Church*, we affirm, that infants being born of holy parents [Lat. *Sanctis.* Fr. *fideles*], are ... to be baptized."[84]

THE HEIDELBERG CATECHISM (Qu. 74) rests on the same view.— "Young children ... by Baptism are separated from the *children of unbelievers.*" In explaining the answer URSINUS[85] says: "All they, and *they alone* are to be baptized, who are disciples of Christ, that is, who *are*, and who ought to be considered members of the *visible* Church, whether they be adults professing faith and repentance, or be *infants* born in

---

[82] Art. XXIII. Ed. Augusti, 166. Niemeyer, 354. Hall's Harm. of Conf. 297.

[83] Ed. Augusti, 72. Niemeyer, 518.

[84] Art. xxxv. Ed. Augusti, 123. Niemeyer, 325, 338. Hall's Harm. Conf. 307.

[85] Corpus Doctrinae, 1612, 441.

the Church: for all the children *of the faithful* are in the covenant, and in the Church of God, unless they exclude themselves. Hence, also, they are disciples of Christ, because they are born iu the Church, which is the school of Christ."

THE CONFESSION OF BELGIA (1566).— "We do detest the error of the Anabaptists, who ...do also condemn the Baptism of infants, yea, of those that be born of *faithful parents*."[86]

THE CANONS OF THE SYNOD OF DORT (Art. I. xvii.).— "Inasmuch as we are to judge of the will of God from His Word, which testifies that the children of *the faithful* are holy, not indeed by nature, but by the benefit of the gracious covenant in which they are comprehended with their parents; *godly* parents ought not to doubt of the election and salvation of *their* children, whom God calls out of this life in their infancy."

DICKSON (Professor of Divinity in the University of Edinburgh) d. 1662 — "Do not the Anabaptists err, who maintain, That no infants, though born of *believing parents* ought to be baptized? Yes, ... To *some* infants of *believers*, as well as to others come to age, the Spirit of Christ hath been given."[87]

In regard to the overwhelming majority of the children not only of the race, but of nominal Christendom, Calvinism holds, therefore, that they are not proper subjects of Baptism, and so far concedes much to the Anabaptists practically, and in regard to each particular case of those to whom it grants Baptism, concedes that it cannot prove, that before God this Baptism is valid, or that it is attended with any value whatever. Calvinism grants, that it does not know, in any one case, that the Baptism of an infant is

---

[86] Art. xxxvi. Ed. Augusti, 193. Niemeyer, 384. Beck, I. 326. Hall's Harm, of Conf. 308.

[87] Truth's Victory. Glasgow, 1772, p. 253.

more than a form, and grants that in no case does Baptism, even as an ordinary means, condition or bear upon the salvation of a child. What more could it grant to Anabaptism without granting everything?

§ 25. CHILDREN OP UNBELIEVERS —REPROBATE INFANTS.

Calvinism not only excludes the children of unbelievers from Baptism, but excludes them as a body from salvation.

CALVIN.[88] — "When the Lord rejects him (the godless man) *with his offspring*, there is certainly no expostulation which we can make with God... If He therefore rejects any one, is it not of *necessity* that such *an one's seed should also be accursed?* ... This therefore is to be held *for certain*, that all who are deprived of the grace of God, are included under the *sentence of eternal death*, whence it follows, that *the children of the reprobate*, whom *the curse of God follows, are subject to the y same sentence.*"

THE BREMEN THEOLOGIANS AT DORT.[89] — "Believers' infants *alone*, who die before they reach the age in which they can receive instruction, do we suppose, to be *loved* of God, and *saved*, of His ... good pleasure."

THE THREE BELGIC PROFESSORS, Polyander, Thyseus, and Walæus, at Dort.[90]— "Infants born of *parents not in the covenant*, the Scripture pronounces impure and aliens from the covenant of grace."

SIBRAND LUBBERT, at the same Synod, gives his decision in these words.— "There is an election of infants, there is a reprobation of infants ... To the infants of the *Church* belongs the promise ... To the

---

[88] On Isaiah xiv. 21, Opera, III.
[89] Acta Synod. Dordr. Judic. 63.
[90] Acta Syn. Dordr. 10.

others (infants), who are out of the Church, no promise is made." To this judgment the three Belgic Professors attach their names as approvers[91]

FRANCIS GOMAR, at the same Synod, treating of "the Special Reprobation of men to damnation," lays down, as *false*, the thesis that "no one is reprobated, no one is damned, on account of original sin alone: consequently there is no reprobation of infants." To this GOMARUS replies: "On account of original sin alone, there is also damnation, which is the wages of every sin, even of sin which is not actual. Therefore also the infants unregenerate, the infants of unbelievers, who are aliens from the covenant of God, are by nature children of wrath, without Christ, without *hope*, without God, as also the infants of the world of the ungodly, in the flood, and the infants of the impious Sodomites, in the burning, perished, and were justly subjected to the wrath of God with their parents."

MARCKIUS.[92] — "Nor is it to be doubted that among these *reprobated* are to be referred ... the *infants of unbelievers*. For though of *individual persons* ... of infants born of unbelievers, we cannot and do not wish particularly to determine, because of God's liberty, and the often secret ways of His Spirit, yet all these are by nature children of wrath, impure, alien, and remote from God, without hope, and left to themselves. God has revealed nothing as decreed or to be done for their salvation, and they are destitute of the ordinary means of grace. So that we ought *utterly to reject, not only their salvation* of which Pelagians dream, but also the Remonstrant (Arminian) theory *that their penalty is one of privation, without sensation.* The terminus to which these are predestined is *eternal death*, destruction, *damnation.* Hence it is fitting to style this the end or

---

[91] Do. 20.
[92] Comp. Theol. Christianae. Amsteloed. 1722, VII. xxxiii. Xxxiv.

terminus, alike of the reprobation and of the creation in time, of the reprobate."

§ 26. THE SECRET IMPEDIMENT.

The Calvinistic system holds that there is a *secret* impediment to the grace of Baptism, in the case of non-elect infants.

MUSCULUS.[93] — "There are impediments which prohibit the grace of Baptism from having place. They are of two kinds: one *secret*, the other open. The *secret* impediment is, if any one belong not to the number of the *elect*, but is of the reprobate, *this impediment* forever prevents participation of the grace of Christ."

Hence the Baptism of *elect*, and of reprobate infants, is made indiscriminate to keep the *secret* from us.

MUSCULUS.[94] — "In the Church of Christ it cannot be observed that only the elect should be baptized. It is as in the Old Testament, in which God Himself so instituted the initial sacrament, as unwilling that in its administration a *discrimination* should be made *by human presumption* between the elect and the reprobate. Nay, He hath so *preserved to Himself* the knowledge of *this discrimination* that He commanded the sacrament of His grace to be administered to all *infants*, the *reprobate* as well as the elect, to Esau, whom He hated in his mother's womb, as well as to Jacob, whom He loved before he was born."

§ 27. NON-ELECT INFANTS HAVE NO RIGHT TO BAPTISM.

Hence non-elect infants have not strictly a right to be baptized, and if they could be known it would be wrong to baptize them.

---

[93] Loci Communes. Basilioe. 1599, 336.
[94] Loci.

CALVIN.[95]— "God, by the secret grace of His Spirit, causes that they (sacraments) shall not be without effect *in the elect.* To *the reprobate* they are merely dead and useless figures."

GRYNÆUS. — "They who have been baptized with water only, not also with the Holy Spirit and fire, ought to be regarded as *not baptized.*"

ZANCHIUS.[96]— "In the Confession of the Church of Strasbourg, 1539, in Article XVIII., the preachers are admonished, that they baptize no one, except this sentence be either *expressed* or *understood*: 'I baptize this person, O God, in accordance with Thy election, and the purpose of Thy Will.'"

WITSIUS.[97]— "If the *most strict* right of Baptism be considered, it *belongs only* to the elect in the verity of the thing, and in the judgment of God, which is ever in conformity with the truth. For inasmuch as Baptism is a sign and seal of that covenant in which He makes over to those who are in His covenant, the goods of saving grace, which have also a sure connection with eternal life, it follows that they who have no right to the goods of the covenant, and never are to have any, have no right before the tribunal of God to the seal of the covenant. The administrators of sacred things, who are to act in the individual cases, from the sole judgment of charity, *know not to distinguish the elect from the non-elect;* and thus far sin not, if also perchance they confer baptism on those to whom in strict right it is not due."

GERDES[98] — "The legitimate subjects of baptism are *the elect* and believing alone, since the good things of the covenant can be sealed to those only for whom they are designed, and to whom they actually come."

---

[95] On Rom. IV. 11. Opera, VII.
[96] Opera, vii. 286.
[97] De efficac. Baptismi in infantib. Misc. Sacr. II. 617.
[98] Doctrina Gratiæ. Duisburg. 1744, 342.

It is evident, then, that on the Calvinistic hypothesis, in Baptism the great name of the adorable Trinity is invoked upon what is always uncertain and sometimes false. Zanchius, to avoid so shocking a possibility, favored the idea that infants should always be baptized *conditionally*, the condition expressed or implied in Baptism being that it was according to the election and purpose of God.[99]

§ 28. CALVINISM WITHOUT A LOGICAL ARGUMENT AGAINST ANABAPTISM.

Calvinism has therefore no logical ground against the *Anabaptist* rejection of infant Baptism.

Calvin[100] — "If an *Anabaptist* were disputing with you, I think *no other* defense would avail you, than this, that they, with justice are received to Baptism whom God has adopted *before they were born*, and to whom He has promised to be a Father. For *unless* God transmit His grace from fathers to sons, to receive new-born infants into the Church would be a mere *profanation of Baptism*."

BEZA.[101] — "No one is to be adorned with the symbol of the family of the Lord, except we suppose that he is *probably* to be counted in that family."

TREMELLIUS AND BEZA'S New Testament.[102] — "Children of believers are indeed, by virtue of the covenant, holy before Baptism, but Baptism comes in, as it were, a seal of holiness."

CLAUBURG.[103] — "The principle is constantly to be maintained, that Baptism *does not confer* on infants

---

[99] Quot. in Limborch Th. Chr. III. V., probably the passage we have quoted: Opera, vii. 286.
[100] Contra Westphal. p. 792. Col. 2.
[101] Vol. I ad defens et Respons Castillibnis, 502.
[102] On I Cor. VII. 14.
[103] Quoted by Witsius. Mis. Sac. II. 633.

the becoming *sons and heirs* of God; but because they are *already* esteemed in that place and in that rank, before God, the grace of adoption is sealed in their flesh by Baptism. *Otherwise* the *Anabaptists would rightly* forbid their Baptism. Unless the *verity* of the outward sign belongs to them, to call them to a participation of the sign itself would be a mere profanation."

BURMANN.[104]— "The power of sacraments is *not to effect* and *produce* a thing, but to signify and seal it." "God is wont to bestow His grace *before* the sacraments are received—of which grace, when they are received, they are but the signs and tokens."

To the *Anabaptists* the Calvinist says: We agree with you that the great mass of infants are not entitled to Baptism; we agree with you that Baptism in no case confers anything objective on the child; the only question between us is, whether the hypothetical sign of a hypothetical condition shall be given them? As God, according to the illustration of Witsius, sometimes sets his seal to blank paper, or paper so scribbled upon that nothing intelligible can be written upon it, and hides from us all of the paper except the place of the seal, and as the value of the seal as a seal all turns upon the contents of the paper, a Calvinistic seal amounts to little more than an engraver's specimen; and, inasmuch as the paper with the true covenant written on it, is just as valid, according to Calvinism, without the seal as with it, the seal seems to be of very little account in any case. Baptism is no more than a seal at most; the seal of empty or blotted paper, in many cases; the seal, at best, of a covenant, to whose force it contributes nothing; a covenant which in no sense is made by it; a covenant which stands in equal force without it. It is hardly worthwhile for Calvinism, on such a basis, to hold out against Anabaptism. It is therefore not without internal

---

[104] Synops VII. IV. XXVIII.

reason that the Calvinistic tendency so often ran out, originally into Anabaptism, that it became a proverb, "a young Calvinist, an old Anabaptist;" that the Anabaptist theories so largely prevail on Calvinistic soils; that the immense growth of the Baptist Church in modern times has taken place where Calvinism has been in the ascendant; that so many Calvinists have become Baptists; that so many Baptists are Calvinists, and that in the Calvinistic churches there is so great and growing a neglect of infant Baptism.

§ 29. THE MEANS OF GRACE IN THEIR RELATION TO INFANTS.

Calvinism acknowledges that there are no *ordinary* means for the salvation of infants.

WESTMINSTER CONFESSION XIV. 1: "The grace of faith ... is *ordinarily* wrought by the ministry of the *Word*: by which also, and by the administration of the sacraments and prayer, it is increased and strengthened." Here it is implied that the Word, read or heard, is the sole means by which grace is *ordinarily* wrought.

Calvinism allows of no potency of the Word except a didactic one (XIV. 2): the sacraments "*and prayer*" *increase* faith but they do not *produce* it.

There is, then, no *ordinary* means for working that faith in infants, without which grace of faith it is acknowledged by Calvinists they cannot be saved. All infants' salvation comes, therefore, into the sphere of the extraordinary, is without means, and requires unmediated divine operations.

THE POSITION OF CHILDREN AN AFTER-THOUGHT. This is largely connected with and solved by the more general fact, that Calvinism makes no proper position for infants in its system, but brings them in by after-thought.

WESTMINSTER CONFESSION, XXV. 2: "*The visible*

Church ... consists of all those throughout the world that profess the true religion, *together with* their children."

This seems to assert that children of professors are *ipso facto* members of the visible Church—and this the Calvinistic theologians constantly maintain. *Profession* of the true religion puts one set of its members into the visible Church—natural birth of these professors puts another set into it—but no unregenerate human being is introduced by God into His visible Church—the sower of the *tares* is always the devil. Those who are in the visible Church in real conformity with God's appointment are also *ipso facto* part of the invisible Church. But in Calvinism the law of natural descent sows tares continually in the visible Church, bringing into it non-elect children, the children of unworthy professors as a class, and often the children of the elect themselves, non-elect children of the elect.

Westminster Confession XXVIII. 1: "Baptism is ... ordained ... for the solemn admission of the party baptized into the visible Church."

The contradiction here seems palpable. The Confession XXV. 2, asserts that the Church consists, in part, of the *children* of professors, and again asserts, XXVIII. 1, that Baptism solemnly *admits* them into the visible Church—that is, the Church in part *consists* of those who have not been admitted into it—and those are admitted into it of whom it already consists—or are there two admissions, one solemn, the other not solemn? The conflict is too palpable to have escaped the notice of Calvinistic divines. BOSTON[105] quoted and endorsed by Dr. Shaw[106] harmonizes the two thus: Baptism "does not *make* them members of the visible Church, but *admits* them solemnly thereto ... for the infants of believing parents ... are Christians and visible

---

[105] Complete Body of Divinity, III. 307.
[106] Exposition of the Confession, 7th Ed. Edinburgh.

Church members"—that is *after* the Church consists of them, *after* they are Christians and *after* they are members, they are solemnly *admitted* to the Church. The real solution seems to us to be this, that infants were not thought of at this point. The writer had adults alone in his eye. But this belief, if it be accepted, confirms our view, that infants are with difficulty brought into the Calvinistic system—as indeed they are into any system which on the one side denies Pelagianism and on the other the objective force of Baptism. It shows that baptism in the case of infants, and in that of adults rests on exactly opposite constructions: You baptize adults because Baptism admits them to the Church; you baptize infants because they are already in the Church.

"It tends greatly," says CUNNINGHAM, "to introduce obscurity and confusion into our whole conceptions upon the subject of Baptism, that we see it ordinarily administered to infants, and very seldom to adults. This leads us insensibly to form very defective and erroneous conceptions of its design and effect, or rather to live with our minds very much in the state of blanks, so far as concerns any distinct and definite views upon the subject. There is a difficulty felt ... in laying down any very distinct and definite doctrine as to the precise bearing and efficacy of Baptism in the case of infants, to whom alone ordinarily we see it administered. And hence it becomes practically, as well as theoretically important to remember, that Ave ought to form our primary and fundamental conceptions of Baptism from the Baptism of *adults* ... It is manifest, that the general doctrine or theory with respect to the design and effect of Baptism, ... must undergo some modification in its application to the case of infants. One fundamental position concerning the sacraments is, that they are intended for believers, and, of course, for believers only, unless some *special exceptional case can be made out*, as we are persuaded can be done in the case of infants of believers." "Baptism is described in our Confession (XXVIII. 1), as 'ordained ... to be *unto him* a sign and seal' ... It applies primarily and fully only to the case of adult Baptism." "The fundamental, spiritual blessings on which the salvation of man universally depends,—justification and regeneration by faith—are not conveyed through the instrumentality of the sacraments, but ... on the contrary, they must *already* exist before even Baptism can be lawfully or safely received."[107]

Dr. Cunningham, was not unconscious of the nature of the ground on which he was treading, and acknowledges, to meet the fact, that "these statements may, at first view, appear to be large concessions to those who oppose the lawfullness of the Baptism of infants."[108]

WESTMINSTER CONFESSION VIII. 8: "To *all* those for whom Christ hath purchased redemption, He doth certainly and effectually apply and communicate the same; ... revealing unto them, in and by the Word, the mysteries of salvation; effectually persuading them ... to believe and obey; and governing their hearts by this Word." ...

Here in spite of the sweeping "all," there is no consideration of children whatever.

Westminster Confession X. 1: "*All* those whom God hath predestinated unto life ... He is pleased, ... to call by His Word and Spirit ... enlightening their minds spiritually and savingly to understand the things of God."

Here again, in spite of the sweeping "all," infants are not embraced.

---

[107] (See Cunningham; Histor. Theology, 1864. II. 25, 127, 144).
[108] (See Cunningham; Histor. Theology, 1864. II. 25, 127, 144).

Calvinism holds, that elect infants are *justified* infants; and yet defines justification so as to make it impossible to infants. Westminster Confession XI. 1: "Those whom God effectually calleth He also freely justifieth." (Do. vi.) "God did from all eternity decree to justify *all the elect.* Nevertheless, they are not justified until the Holy Spirit doth in due time actually apply Christ unto them."

ELECT infants *may* be in any case justified while they are infants: they *must* be justified while they are infants if they die in infancy. So Calvinism allows. But the whole confessional conception of justification is one which excludes infants.

"They (the justified) receiving and resting on him ... by faith ... Faith *thus* receiving ... is the alone instrument of justification."

The Calvinistic answer is that adults are spoken of, but the answer is the accusation. The accusation is that the conception is one which embraces none but adults, and that conception *alone* is constantly presented.

Calvinism maintains not only the possibility, but the absolute necessity of the *regeneration* of infants, but knows of no means for that regeneration and no assurance of faith that any particular child is regenerate. "Elect infants, dying in infancy are *regenerated,*" (Westminster Confession x.x.) but the conception of regeneration as presented in the Confession makes it inapplicable to infants.

§ 30. CALVINISTIC DOCTRINE OF THE CHURCH IN ITS BEARING ON INFANT SALVATION.

Calvinism holds that out of the invisible Church there is no salvation whatever, and that out of the visible Church there is no ordinary possibility of salvation.

MARTYR. [109] — "It is necessary that they (children) belong unto Christ and the Church, seeing, out of it, there is no salvation."

URSINUS.[110]— "It is required, of necessity, that in this life they (the elect) be brought unto the Church, though it be sometimes even at the very point of death." "*No man* can be saved out of the Church. Whomsoever God hath chosen and elected to the *end*, which is eternal life, them hath He chosen to the *means*; which is the inward and *outward* calling."

VOSSIUS.[111]— "Nor do we exclude the children of unbelievers alone, but the children of those who are open heretics: to whom Baptism should be refused even though it be asked by the parents."

WESTMINSTER CONFESSION X. 4.— "Others not elected . . cannot be saved: much less can men not professing the Christian religion be saved in any other way whatever . . and to assert . . . that they may, is very pernicious, and to be detested." Larger Catechism, Q. 60: "They who, having never heard the Gospel, know not Jesus Christ and believe not in Him, cannot be saved. Christ is the Savior only of His body, the Church." Q. 61: "They only (are saved) who are true members of the Church invisible."

WESTMINSTER CONFESSION XXV. 1.— "The ... church ... *invisible* consists of the whole number of the elect." (Do. ii.)— "The *visible* Church ... is the kingdom of the Lord Jesus Christ, the house and family of God, out of which there is no ordinary possibility of salvation."

These principles in their connections,

1. Clearly exclude the entire heathen, Mohammedan and Jewish world from salvation. It is a

---

[109] Common Places.
[110] Sum of Christian Religion, Lond. 1633, 359, 352. Corpus Doctrinae, 1612. 350, 361, 362.
[111] De Baptism. Disp. xv. p. 190.

Calvinistic article of faith that men not professing the *Christian faith* cannot be saved.

2. Connecting with this the doctrine that as is the state of the parents so is the *presumed* state of the children *individually*, and the *certain* state of the children as a *class*, it follows that the moral *presumption* is that each child of the non-Christian world is lost, and the moral *certainty* is that they are lost as a class. It is certain that not one of them is of the visible church, "out of which there is no ordinary possibility of salvation," and there is no evidence, no reason even, for hope that a single one of them is of the Church invisible.

3. This looks gloomy enough, but there is still another dark point. "The visible Church ... consists of all those that *profess the true religion* (Westminster Confession XXVI. i.) "*The True Religion,*" what is that? Strictly construed, Calvinism—which claims—and must for consistency's sake claim to be "the true religion." Confessions are meant to define "the true religion," in the sense in which those who make and adhere to them define "the true religion." We understand the Westminster Confession to furnish the Presbyterian answer to the question, What is the true religion? Does this then mean to exclude a large part of the children of nominal Christendom, as it does their parents, from the visible Church, from all presumption of election, and all probability of salvation? We are afraid that it does. It has never been so logically pressed as to exclude from hope *all* that are not professed Calvinists, but it has been pressed to the exclusion of Papists, Arminians, and the various bodies of nominally Christian errorists. "The true religion" seems to be synonymous with what is called, XXIV. iii., "the true reformed religion," by which is meant in the Westminster Confession, as the usage and controversies of the time will show, the Calvinistic religion, as over against Romanism,

Lutheranism, and the then dominant doctrinal tendency of the Church of England. It is there said: "It is the duty of *Christians* to marry only in the Lord. And therefore such as profess the true Reformed religion should not marry with infidels, papists, or *other* idolaters."

"Christians" and "such as profess the Reformed religion," are one and the same thing: the inference rests on the assumption of their identity. "Papists" are not "Christians," but are "idolaters," lumped with the "other idolaters" —the major part of nominal Christendom being carried over to the general realm of Juggernaut and Mumbo Jumbo.

The same paragraph further forbids marrying "with such as ... maintain damnable heresies," and of such Christendom unhappily holds not a few. As are the parents, so are the children to be presumed to be; wrong-minded Christendom is out of the Church visible and invisible, so are their children as a class, and as a class presumed to be lost. All Pagandom, all Islam, all the Jews, Roman Christendom, Greek Christendom (by parity of reason), and a large part of the Protestant world, under the Calvinistic construction, moving out of the ordinary possibility of salvation, the children doomed as a class, without the probability, not to say certainty of the salvation of a single one! Surely this is a sufficiently liberal provision for damnation, but is it not open to the charge of being rather a parsimonious one for salvation?

§ 31. CALVINISM AND ROMANISM ON INFANT SALVATION.

In the controversies between Calvinists and Romanists, the attitude of the former on the question of infant damnation is decisive, if there were nothing else, on the question in which Dr. Hodge considers that we have made an assertion without due warrant. The Romanists assert that there is a *Limbus infantum*, a place in the other world in which the souls of un-baptized infants endure the penalty of loss (*damni*), but not of positive suffering (*sensus*). To this the attitude of the classic Calvinistic divines is invariable. It is 1: that elect infants are saved, though unbaptized. 2: that non-elect infants, whether baptized or not, enter not upon a Limbus of loss—a negative damnation, but on a hell of suffering, a positive and eternal damnation. 3: They charge it upon Rome as a Pelagian error, that she softens unduly the state of lost infants.

CALVIN AND PIGHIUS. —One of Calvin's most distinguished Romish opponents was ALBERT PIGHIUS (d. 1543), who wrote against him a work in two books, "Concerning free will and grace." Cologne, 1542. He maintained "that original sin in young children is nothing else but the actual sin of Adam that is imputed to them, and that, properly speaking, there is no blemish in them of inherent sin."[112]

CALVIN[113], in reply to Pighius, says: "If Pighius holds that original sin is not sufficient to damn men, and that the secret council of God is not to be admitted, what will he do with infant children, who, before they have reached an age at which they can give any such specimens ... [as he demands], are snatched from this life ... For inasmuch as the conditions of birth and death were alike to infants who died in Sodom and those who died in Jerusalem: and there were no difference in their works: why will Christ, at the last day, separate some to stand as His right hand, others at His left?"

Calvin assumes as granted, and as undisputed that the infants of Sodom were damned. He appeals to it as a known something to settle a contested point, and after the words we have cited goes on to say: "Who will not adore this wonderful judgment of God whereby it

---

[112] Du Pin's Ecclesiastical History of the Sixteenth Century. Lond., 1710. Vol. I. 427. Herzog, Real. En. XI. 662, XV. 216.
[113] De Æterna Dei Prædes inatione. Tom. VIII. 611.

comes to pass that some are born at Jerusalem, whence soon they pass to a better life, while Sodom, the gates of the lower regions, receives others at their birth?"

Pighus assumed that children have no inherent sin, in order to prove that they ought not to be positively damned. Calvin assumed that children are damned, to strengthen the proof that they have inherent sin. The damnation of infants is the *Pou sto* from which Calvin proposes to move Pighius' world of error. The tone of assurance in the old Calvinistic divines in asserting infant damnation is very striking.

They not only do not doubt the doctrine, but they assume that no man in his senses can doubt it. Not only is an argument not weakened by involving infant perdition, but infant perdition stiffens up an argument otherwise weak. Never was error more effectually driven to bay, in their judgment, than when it was shown that if that error were granted, infant salvation, or even the middle state of Limbus, would follow. The doctrine of infant damnation virtually formed a part of the Calvinistic analogy of faith.

CHAMIER AGAINST THE ROMANISTS. —The name of CHAMIER (d. 1621) is one of the greatest, not only among Calvinistic divines, but in all theological literature. His Panstratiæ Catholicæ (1626) is the ablest work from a Calvinistic hand in the great Roman Catholic Controversy, and takes its general rank with books like Chemnitz's Examen and Gerhard's Confessio Catholica. It was prepared at the request of the Synod of Larochelle.[114] There is no difference of opinion among competent judges as to its distinguished merits, and it is justly regarded among all Calvinists as one of the highest authorities. The word "Catholic," in the title of Chamier's book, and throughout, is used in its Protestant sense, as equivalent to "Christian," or

---

[114] Herzog's Real-Encycl. II. 632. Bayle's Dict. Art. Chamier.

"Orthodox," and by the "Catholics," Chamier means especially the "Calvinists." It is the "Catholics" against the "Papists," who appear in this book. In his discussion of the "penalty of original sin,"[115] Chamier first states the views of the Papists, as three-fold: 1. "That infants (dying in original sin) are excluded from the kingdom of heaven; yet enjoy outside of it a certain natural blessedness." 2. "That those who die in original sin only, are not happy, yet endure no pain, or '*penalty* of sense' (*pœnam sensus*), but are punished only with the penalty of loss (*pœna damni*), that is, are deprived of the vision of God." 3. "Others liberate them from that torment (Mark ix.) 'in which the worm dieth not,' but affirm that the loss of blessedness will be accompanied by internal pain, so that their penalty will be one both of loss and of sense." Bellarmine regards the third as the most probable, but the majority of the Roman Catholic divines accept the second.

In opposition to these mitigating constructions Chamier declares "the Catholics" (Calvinists) maintain that infants also, guilty of original sin, are by God's just sentence damned (*reos solius originalis peccati, justa Dei sententia damnari*): and that in that damnation they are not merely exiled from the kingdom of heaven, but in very deed suffer that eternal fire which is appointed for the devil and his angels ("*re veri pati ignem æternum, assignation diabolo et Angelis ejus.*") * * "There is not merely a privation of eternal blessedness, but also real pains in hell, loss conjoined with sense." For the soundness of these positions Chamier argues at great length.

MARESIUS AGAINST THE ROMANISTS. —Another of the greatest names, in high renown for ability and

---

[115] Chamierus Contractus sive Panstratiæ Catholic. D. Charaieri theologi summi Epitome. Opera Fr. Spanheim. Genev. 1643. Fol. 797, 798.

Calvinistic orthodoxy, is that of MARESIUS (d. 1673).[116] He has been called the Calvinistic Calovius. His life was a life of contest against the errors outside of Calvinism, and errors which tried to shelter themselves within it. His greatest work is in his reply to Tirinus, the Jesuit, who had added to his Commentary (1632) an "Index of Controversies on Matters of Faith." Maresius first gives Tirinus in full, in his own words, and then adds his own strictures. Tirinus says, speaking of the " punishment of original sin:" "In the other life, original sin, for example, in the case of infants who by it are unfitted for that life, is punished eternally. First, by a mournful want of the society of the Saints, and of the vision and fruition of God. Second, by a want of natural blessedness * * they are in prison, light and pleasant indeed, yet of the nature of hell (*infernali*), in which, under the power of the devil, they dwell to eternity."

The completest answer to Tirinus, had it been possible on Calvinistic grounds, would have been a denial that infants are lost at all—there is no limbus for them—they pass, without exception, to heaven. But the answer of Maresius is exactly the opposite: there is no limbus for lost infants, nothing but hell. Maresius[117] says: "There are two rocks to be avoided here: For I. We do not think that the children of the faithful * * who die before baptism, are to be excluded from the kingdom of heaven." II. The punishment of those (children) who are not received into the kingdom of heaven, we hold to be eternal death, not merely that of loss (in the Socinian or Papal sense), but also of sense; hence, we rightly reject that third place which our adversaries call the Limbus of children, for 1. Eternal death is the wages of every

---

[116] Pfaff, etc. Herzog: Real-Encyl. Art. Maresius. Bayle's Dictionary: Do. Walch Einleit., in Rel. Str. auss. d. Ev. Luth. Kirchen. Th. 479.

[117] Theologiæ Elenchticæ Nova Synopsis. Groningæ, 16-18. 2 V. 4to, I. 539.

kind of sin, and therefore of original sin, and so ought to be the portion of those" (children) "who are shut out from heaven arid eternal life. 2. There are two paths only—one goes to life and heaven, the other to perdition and hell. 3. Into the outer darkness where there is weeping and gnashing of teeth—not into a '*light* and *pleasant*' prison, as Tirinus feigns—are they cast who are not admitted to the joys of heaven. 4. They who are not wheat, are assigned to unquenchable fire. To feign a middle order, who are neither wheat nor chaff—neither elect nor reprobate— neither redeemed nor unredeemed by Christ—what is this but to rave? 5. If even the infants who are redeemed by Christ, and who are to be saved in heaven, are not free from temporal death and those pains and miseries which are penalties of nature, why should we exempt *from the pains of hell even as to sense, those*" (*infants*) "*whom Christ did not redeem*, and of whom he sustained neither the persons nor penalties on the cross. 7. This view was the invention of Pelagius and the ancient Pelagians. 8. It is opposed to the view of Augustine and of his followers."

Maresius then cites passages from Augustine and his disciples which teach that unbaptized infants, even those who are unbaptized because they die unborn, are to "be punished with the everlasting torment of eternal fire" (*ignus æterni sempiterno supplicio puniendos*). Maresius, after quoting these passages in his own behalf against Tirinus, says that "Augustine and his followers erred in seeming to bind the justifying, regenerating and sanctifying grace of Christ to the outward sacrament of Baptism," and then adds: "but what they hold, that *infants*, the guilt of whose original sin God has not remitted for Christ's sake, and whom he has not washed from the stain of it through the grace of regeneration, *are, in common with other reprobates, to undergo the punishment of eternal*

*death is most true "(quod statuunt poenam mortis æternæ
cum aliis reprobis subituros infantes ... est verissimum).*"

And even when Calvinism began to reveal a
mitigating tendency, it still held for a long time firmly
to the idea, over against the Pelagianism, as it
considered it, of the Church of Rome, that non-elect
infants are damned.

On the question: "Whether original sin of its
own nature merits *eternal damnation,* or simply
excludes from the kingdom of heaven, and deprives of
the beatific vision unbaptized infants?" Lampe [118]
asserts the former, over against the Roman Catholics
who maintain the latter.

RESULT. We write it with sorrow, but truth
compels us to say that on this point the Calvinistic
doctrine is far more shocking than that of the Roman
Catholic Church, for it casts upon the thousands even
of baptized children the shadow of doubt, substituting
in the best cases a mere charitable presumption, for a
firm assurance, and outside of these, leaves to eternal
privation and eternal misery, the great mass of dying
infants who are *not* "children of the faithful."

§ 32. CALVINISM AND PELAGIANISM.

Calvinism constantly maintains the doctrine of
infant damnation, as essential to a consistent position
against Pelagianism. This point has already been made,
in other connections, in a number of our quotations. It
would be easy to add to them.

STAPFER. —Stapfer[119] states the ninth objection
of the *Pelagians* in these terms: "To subject infants to
eternal punishments because of Adam's sin would be to
deal more severely with them than with the devil
himself, or with Adam, who himself committed sin." In

---

[118] Rudimenta Theolog. Elenchticae, Bremæ, 1729, p. 55.
[119] Institut. Theolog. polemic. Tiguri, 1716, IV. 517.

his reply to this, Stapfer says: "As to the children of unbelievers we believe that they will be separated from the communion of God, and hence in the very fact that as children of wrath and cursing, they are excluded from the beatific communion of God, *they will be damned.*"

CALVIN AGAINST SERVETUS.

The controversy with Servetus comes into the same general line of argument, and may therefore properly be introduced here.

The whole body of Genevan pastors, fifteen in number, with Calvin heading the list,[120] charge upon Servetus, as one of his errors—the errors which cost him his life—that he asserts that

"he dare condemn none of the (infant) offspring of Ninevites or Barbarians to hell (*futurum gehennam*) because, in his opinion, a merciful Lord, who hath freely taken away the sins of the godless, would never so severely condemn those by whom no godless act has been committed, and who are most innocent images of God," and further he infers that "all who are taken from life as infants and children are exempt from eternal death, though they be elsewhere called accursed."[121]

§ 33. CALVINISM AND ARMINIANISM, ON THE ELECTION AND REPROBATION OF INFANTS, AND THE INSANE. CASTALIO, THE FORERUNNER OF ARMINIANISM.

CALVIN AGAINST CASTALIO. CALVIN[122] wrote with great bitterness against CASTALIO, who had been

---

[120] Refutatio Errorum Michaelis Serveti, Opera, Tom. VIII. 559.
[121] Do. do. 597.
[122] De occulta Dei Providentia (1558), Opera. Amstelodam. 1667. Tom. VIII. 644, 645.

his friend, but who speedily showed the working of the tendencies which matured at a later period unto Arminianism:

"You deny that it is lawful for God, except for misdeed, to condemn any human being. Nevertheless numberless infants are removed from life. Put forth now your virulence against God, who precipitates into eternal death harmless new-born children (*innoxios foetus*) torn from their mother's bosoms. Your masters, Servetus, Pighius, and such like dogs (*similes canes*), say at least that before the world was created some were condemned whom God foreknew worthy of destruction. But you will not concede that He devotes to eternal death any except those who for perpetrated evil deeds would be exposed to penalty under earthly judges ...You do not hesitate to overturn the whole order of divine justice."

It is in meeting objectors of the school of Castalio, CALVIN says:[123] "Whence hath it come that the fall of Adam hath involved in eternal death so many nations with their infant children without remedy, unless, because it so pleased God? Here the tongues that have been so voluble it becomes to be mute. That the decree is fearful, I confess: yet no man can deny that God foreknew before He created him what end man should have; and foreknew it because He had so ordained it by His decree." "There are those born among men, devoted from the womb to certain death, who by their destruction glorify God's name."[124]

ARMINIUS. —When the element of opposition to Calvinism, which had smoldered in it from its beginning, broke into a light flame in Arminius (1560-1609), the damnation of infants was one of the first points of assault on the one side, of firm, repeated

---

[123] Institut. Lib III. XXIII. 7. Opera, IX. 254. Compared with Fetherstone's Translation, Edinburgh, 1587.

[124] Do. do. 6.

statements and defense on the other. The fiercer struggle which followed the death of Arminius, is full of illustrations of the unrelenting tenacity with which Calvinism held as essential to sound doctrine the reality of infant reprobation and of infant damnation. Arminius, the pupil of Beza, who was Calvin's greatest scholar, and of Grynæus, was high in repute in the Church of Holland, and in 1604 as successor of Junius, became Professor of Theology in the University of Leyden, and received from the hand of Gomarus the Doctorate. Chosen to defend the system of Calvin and Beza, his more careful examination of the system led him to reject it. His learning and his mildness are beyond all dispute. His desire was not to magnify the points of difference between himself and the Calvinists, but to reduce them in bulk, and to soften them in tone as much as possible. In 1608 he was summoned before the Orders of Holland, and commanded explicitly to state his views on the doctrines in dispute. In stating the views of the Calvinistic divines, which he controverted "as they are embraced everywhere (*passim*) in their own writings," he notes that they hold that "the children of the faithful and holy, God leads to salvation by a shorter way (than this of adults), if they depart this life before they come to riper years; *that is to say, if so be (nimirum siquidem) they belong to the number of the elect (whom God alone knoweth)*."

"The means of the execution of reprobation to eternal death pertains in part to *all the rejected and reprobate* (whether they reach adult life or *die before they reach it*), partly to some only. The means common to the whole is *desertion*; the means peculiar to some is hardening."[125]

---

[125] The defense is given in full in Jägers: Hist. Eccles. Sec. dec. Sept. Tubingae. 1691. Ann. 1608, pp. 301-328.

THE CONTRA – REMONSTRANT (CALVINISTIC) RESPONSE. 1611.

The statement of Arminius as to the Calvinistic doctrine of infant reprobation was never denied—on the contrary every reference to it shows that there was no disposition to dispute its correctness. The doctrine might be palliated in the mode of statement, but as to the fact involved the Calvinists and Arminians do not differ. The Calvinists in their Response, 1611, say:

"As elect of God are also to be esteemed (*habendos*) ... the children of the covenant, so long as they do not in fact (*reipsa*) *demonstrate the contrary*, wherefore, faithful parents should not doubt concerning the salvation of their children, when they die in infancy."

This is the theory we constantly meet with: First, that it is to be *presumed* that all the children of the elect are elect; second, that the presumption is often shown to be groundless by the after life of these children; third, that this presumption, often fallacious and never certain, is the only refuge of parents who love their children—they are presumed to be elect, and as they die before they can "in fact demonstrate the contrary," the presumption, such as it is, is left in full force.

§ 34. THE SYNOD OF DORT.

The National Synod of Dort, 1618, 1619, was meant, if possible, to unite the entire Calvinistic Churches against the common foe. At the outstart it was not so much Arminians who charged Calvinists with teaching infant reprobation and damnation, as it was Calvinists, who charged on Arminians, as a deadly error, that their principles legitimately led to a denial of this doctrine, though the Arminians had not yet consistency or courage enough distinctly to make the denial in an unreserved form. For so strong was the current of Calvinism in regard to infant reprobation and infant damnation, that even the *Remonstrant Arminians* could not directly set themselves wholly against it. The Arminians at first acknowledged a sort of negative hell for some infants (the *poena damni*), and the Calvinists, over against this, argue for a positive one (the *poena sensus*). Over against this Arminian tendency, even with this softening and spirit of concession, the utterances of the divines at Dort were of the most decided kind. Infant reprobation, and the actual damnation of infants, were asserted in manifold shapes, and in all the public discussions of that body no Calvinist of any land uttered a word of doubt or of mitigation. There were points on which differences were expressed, there were feelings aroused which threatened the very continuance of the Synod, but there was a happy harmony in regard to infant reprobation.

THE SYNOD OF DORT ON THE BAPTISM OF PAGAN INFANTS.

—At the Eighteenth and Nineteenth Sessions (Dec. 1, 3, 1619,) the question of the Baptism of the infants of heathen who came under Christian control was discussed. At the Twenty-first Session (Dec. 5) it was determined: "that they should by no means (*nullo modo*) be baptized before they attained years of discretion."[126]

THE OFFICIAL JUDGMENT SET FORTH BY THE ARMINIANS AT DORT. —At the Twenty-third Session, Dec. 23, 1619, the Sententia, or Official Judgment on Predestination signed by all the Remonstrant divines present, was read by Episcopius. Two articles in it ran

---

[126] Author Anon—qui interfuit Synodo. Given in Jäger, H. E. 1619, 314. Brandt, III. 37. In the Acta Synodi I. 49., the decision is given under Session XIX.

thus;

IX.: "*All* the children of the faithful are sanctified in Christ, so that *not one* of them, dying before the use of reason, perishes; *in no wise,* on the contrary, are even *some* of the children of the faithful, dying in infancy, before any sin of act (*actuale*) committed in their own person, to be counted in the number of the reprobate, so that neither the holy laver of Baptism, nor the prayers of the Church can in any way profit them to salvation."

How sharp and clear is the antithesis. The Calvinists hold that *some* of the infants of the faithful, to wit, the elect children, are sanctified; the Arminians declare that *all* are; the Calvinists hold that *some* infants of the faithful perish; the Arminians declare that *none* do; the Calvinists taught that there were infants, to wit, reprobate infants, to whom neither Baptism nor the prayers of the Church brought saving blessing. The Arminians declare that there is no such class of infants.

But the Arminians saw that the constant hypothecating of the *death* of the *infants* left the vital center of the question untouched. On the Calvinistic side such a hypothecating seemed to imply that the death of the infant in some way influenced its election; whereas, in fact, on the Calvinistic theory the child's death has nothing to do with its election. An absolute election does not take into regard the death of the infant at all. If the *adult* life of the children of the elect shows, that many infants of the elect, who live, are among the reprobate, it equally shows, that many infants of the elect who die are among the reprobate, for the two classes are exactly alike before an absolute decree. *All Calvinists,* even those of the gentle type of Dr. Hodge, are compelled to acknowledge that there are *non-elect or reprobate infants*; that is, that the non-elect or reprobate are such always; such though unborn; such at their birth; and through their whole infancy.

Only the milder class hold, that such infants always grow up to the age of responsibility—no non-elect infants ever die, according to this new school of Calvinism. It has found out part of God's secret of fore-ordination. It is, that infant death is the seal of infant election; the death of the infant is the true sacrament of its adoption—Baptism is not. The Arminians met the fallacious hypothecating in their next article, which reads thus:

"*No children* of believers baptized in the name of the Father, and of the Son, and of the Holy Spirit, while they are *living* in the state of infancy, are to be counted among those who have been reprobated by an absolute decree."[127]

It will be noticed, that the Arminians confine their statement to the "children of the *faithful*" but these, *when baptized, in no case*, equally if they *live*, as if they die, are to be counted among the reprobate. With the Word of God, with pure antiquity, and with an overwhelming majority of the Church of Christ in all ages, the Augustinian portion, no less heartily than the others, the Arminians, regarded Baptism in a light in which Calvinism completely anti-Augustinian here, cannot regard it, as the evidence in the infant of a present state of grace.

A recent writer[128] has praised Calvin for denying, that infants dying unbaptized are *ipso facto* lost. That was well in Calvin, so far, but that writer has failed to note that just in proportion as Calvin weakens the assumption that non-baptism proves that a child is lost, he weakens the faith that a baptized child is saved—that if non-baptism is no evidence of a child's damnation, baptism is no evidence of its salvation. Calvin's theory involves the certain damnation of the

---

[127] Acta Synodi, 113. Brandt, III. 84.
[128] Lecky: Rationalisim in Europe. Rev. Edit. New York, 1872, I. 367.

majority of the infants of the race, and does not claim that there is distinct evidence even in the most hopeful case that any particular child is saved. It does not widen the probability of infant salvation, as Lecky supposes, but narrows it. It does not exalt infant salvation, but simply lowers Baptism.

THE ARMINIAN CHALLENGE. —The Arminians urged an explicit reply: "It has been given out among the common people that we have ... falsely represented the doctrines of the Contra-remonstrants... If this be true, let them as plainly and flatly renounce those doctrines as we do."[129] "We especially (*unice*) desire to know from this venerable Synod, whether it acknowledges as its own doctrine and the doctrine of the Church, particularly (*nominatim*) what is asserted ... concerning the creation of the larger part of mankind for destruction, the *reprobation of infants even though born of believing parents.*"[130]

So simple and direct a challenge could properly allow of but two answers. One would have been "the views of infant reprobation, you reject, we reject also." The other would have been, "the views you reject, we maintain." The answers at Dort all rest on the second position, and are expressed in far stronger terms than the Arminians had employed. They state the views from which the Arminians dissent.

DORT IS POLITIC. —There is, however, a marked difference between two classes of utterance in the Synod of Dort. Those that were meant for the great public are cautious and illusive in the framing. The truth was too palpable to be denied, nor did the men of Dort desire to deny it, but they wished to avoid the odium of unmitigated statement. On the contrary, the statements meant for the Synod itself, and for its

---

[129] Acta, 119. Brandt, III. 190
[130] Acta, 121. Brandt, III. 93.

theologians, are clear, sharp, and cruel.

Of the former class, is its First Canon:[131]

"XVII. Inasmuch as we must judge of the will of God from His Word, which testifies that the children of the faithful are holy, not indeed by nature, but by benefit of the gracious covenant, wherein they, together with their parents, are comprised, *godly* parents ought not to doubt of the election and salvation of their children whom God calls out of this life in their infancy."

The impression produced by these words on a plain reader, divested of the key to their sense, is entirely illusive. He sees indeed that they imply that the infants of pagans, Jews and all non-Christians are lost; that they offer no hope to the infants of merely nominal Christians, and that within the Calvinistic Church itself they confine the hope to the children of the "faithful," of believers, of those "comprised within the gracious covenant," "the godly." They mean therefore that within the visible Church itself there is no hope in regard to the great mass of children. But the plain reader will perhaps need to be told that though we "*must* judge of the will of God from *His Word*," Calvinistic theology rests on a "will of God" which is not revealed in His Word, what the Westminster Confession (III. iv.) calls "the *secret* counsel and good pleasure of His will," and that this is the very will involved in the election of infants. The plain reader may need to be told that the " holiness" of the children of the faithful, of which Dort speaks, is one which involves of necessity neither change of nature nor

---

[131] Acta, 252. The Canons are given in Latin in Augusti. Corpus, Lib. Symb. Eccles. Reform. Elberfeld, 1827, 198-240. Niemeyer: Collect. Confess. Lipsiæ, 1840, 690-728. They are given in English in Hall's Harmony of Confessions. Lond. 1844, 539-573; in German in Beck's Sammlung Symb. Buecher. Neustadt. 1845, I. 344.

election, but exists equally in the cases in which the children of the faithful grow up into manifold reprobacy. If it meant more it would bring the Calvinistic system to the ground, for if *all* the children of believers are regenerate, all of them are elect; and as some of the children of believers die unregenerate, it would follow that some of the elect fell finally from grace, and with their fall, Calvinism itself would fall. It is the old theory over again—a presumption resting on a presumption, and begetting a presumption that some dying infants, nobody knows which, may be saved.

But the disingenuousness of Dort has gone yet further. After giving what it styles "the plain and simple explication of the Orthodox doctrine," it denounces certain allegations of the Remonstrants. One of the charges thus denounced is that Calvinists hold that "many innocent infants of believers are torn from the breasts of their mothers, and tyrannically plunged into hell."[132] The official paper of the Remonstrants published in the acts of the Synod of Dort show that they did not make the charge that Calvinists held that "*many*" infants of believers are lost, but that they disavowed for themselves the doctrine that any are lost, and asked the Synod to express itself clearly on this point. The rhetorical nourish about "innocent infants torn from the breasts of their mothers," was not used by the Remonstrants at all before this Synod. When they used it they simply quoted Calvin. (See "Calvin against Castalio," already quoted).

The real meaning of the evasive words of Dort was at once pointed out by Episcopius as being this: "The reprobate infants of the faithful are not 'innocent,' but guilty, and God in casting them into hell, does not act 'tyrannically,' but exercises only the just rights of a

---

[132] Acta, 275. Augusti: 239. Niemeyer, 722. Hall: 570. Beck: 393.

ruler."[133]

DORT IS CANDID. —The official judgments of the theologians of the various States represented at Dort, fix with the greatest precision the meaning of its Canons, and of the various terms of Calvinistic orthodoxy.

The theologians of Great Britain, in addition to what we have quoted, say: "The thesis that there is no election of infants, in the sense that there is no election between one and the others, as if all were indiscriminately saved, is a hypothesis *without any foundation* whatever to rest on (*nec ullis fundamentis nititur*)." They quote with approval, and as authority, Prosper's words: "There is a distinction made in regard to infants by God's judgment; some are taken as heirs, and others passed by as debtors." [134] The Swiss theologians,[135] the Bremen theologians,[136] as we have seen, wrote in the same vein, and need not be quoted a second time.

The Third Part of the Acts of the Synod of Dort embraces the judgments of the theologians of the provinces. We have given the judgment of the three Belgic Professors,[137] and of Lubbert, and Lubbert signs the paper of the three, and the three sign the paper of Lubbert, as if they could not get enough of signing such delicious documents. We gave Lubbert's Thesis that "some are lost for original sin only." We add the sole proof, which he gives of the Thesis: "This Thesis is proved by the destruction (*interitus*) of *many infants* who die in infancy, out of the Church and out of Christ."—[138]

---

[133] Examen Thesium.
[134] Acta Judicia, 10.
[135] Do. 40, 44.
[136] Do. 63.
[137] Acta, III. 10, 11
[138] Do. 20.

We have also quoted Gomarus.[139] None of these judgments give an uncertain sound on infant damnation. But these are not all. THE DEPUTIES OF THE SYNOD OF SOUTH HOLLAND,[140] mark the points very clearly: "*All infants are liable* (*obnoxiis*) *to eternal damnation*, on account of original sin, and that *reprobation has a place in believers' children also*, who live to adult years, is clearly proved by Holy Scripture and experience. But whether this same (reprobation) has a place also in the infants of believers, who die in infancy, without actual sins, is a question which they (the Deputies) think is not too nicely (*curiose*) to be examined into; but inasmuch as there exist in Holy Scriptures, testimonies which take away from believing parents all occasion (*causam*) of doubting concerning the election and salvation of their infants, they think that these (testimonies) are to be *acquiesced* in." Here comes up again that appalling feature of the old Calvinism—we are to *acquiesce* in the *testimony* of the Word, though the secret counsel may make that testimony an illusion.

THE THEOLOGIANS FROM DRENTHE[141] are no less explicit: "We are now to speak of *infants, under which* (*sub quibus*) *we embrace also adults who have been insane from their birth* (*adultos mente ab exordio vitæ alienatos*), that is to say, of those infants who die in infancy. We give our judgment (*statuimus*) that the infants of unbelievers, dying in infancy, are reprobate... The *infants of believers*, though they die in infancy, could justly be reprobated by God and left in their misery, if God willed to use His right. *Notwithstanding* (*interim*) *faithful* parents can conceive a sure *hope* (*certam spem possunt concipere*) concerning the salvation of such little infants (*infantorum lorum*); for

---

[139] Do. 24, 26.
[140] Do. 39.
[141] Do. 91.

we do not read in Scripture that such were ever reprobated; on the contrary, the Scripture testifies of God's good affection to such."

The infants of the reprobates, dying in infancy, are reprobate, and those who are insane from their birth, are involved in the same principles. These men hold that a part of our race born in insanity, living in insanity, and dying in insanity, are damned, and to this view logical Calvinism can offer no reply.

§ 35. SEVERITY OF THE CALVINISTIC SPIRIT.

The terrible earnestness of the Calvinistic feeling against Arminianism, complicated and inflamed by political animosities, did not exhaust itself in theses, judgments, canons, condemnations and denunciations. The State was for the time a theocratic instrument of the divines. The Arminian congregations were forcibly scattered. They were forbidden to worship God in public. Their professors and pastors were deposed and banished. The banishment was so sudden that those at Dort were not allowed to return to their homes to bid farewell to their loved ones, or to arrange their private affairs. Grotius and Hogerbeets were sentenced to perpetual imprisonment in the castle of Lovestein. Over the dead body of Ledenberg, who had committed suicide to avoid, as it was thought, the terrors of the rack (Sept. 28, 1618) sentence was pronounced May 15, 1619; the body was drawn upon a sledge to the gibbet and hung upon it. The aged statesman and patriot, Olden Barneveldt, one of the founders of the civil liberty of Holland, was beheaded. The awful severity of the character of God, as the Calvinistic system construed it, reflected itself in their conduct toward those whom they regarded as His enemies; the system which held that a babe unborn might justly be subject to eternal pains "without remedy," would not spare the blow which prostrated the men who made battle against the system which involved these views, which Calvinists of that day cherished as the very truth of God.

§ 36. THE CONFESSION AND APOLOGY OF THE ARMINIANS AND THE CALVINISTIC CENSURE.

The "Confession" of the Remonstrants, written 1621, by Episcopius, appeared in 1622. It was answered by four of the Leyden Professors, in a "Censure." The "Censure" drew forth a defense (Apologia) of the Confession from the pen of Episcopius. The Arminian Confession says: "God has prepared in His beloved Son a free remedy for all." To this the Censure replies: "If they mean this, even of all them who *die without actual sin of their* own, we see not how they can deny that they are Pelagians."

In their reply to this the Remonstrants say: "This passage shows that our adversaries believe that *absolute reprobation* pertains not only to the infants of the Gentiles, but is to be extended to the infants of those who are in the covenant, and believers; and, however they may wish to seem in any case to think contrary to this, that is to be understood only of the judgment of charity, not of faith."[142]

The Apology of the Arminians in another passage states the position of the Calvinists as conveyed in this question: "Why shall it be thought absurd or wicked to say, that God not only wills of His good pleasure to destroy, but also to devote to the inner torments of hell the larger part of the human race, many myriads of infants torn from their mothers' breasts? for these are the horrid inferences which the school of Calvin rears on those foundations, which

---

[142] Apologia pro Confessione—contra Censuram, 1630, 4to, 87, 6. (It is significant that neither the name of the printer nor of the place of publication is given.)

consequently the Remonstrants look upon with their whole soul full of aversion and abhorrence."[143]

The Apology of the Arminians was answered by Trigland (1652-1705) in his Antapologia.[144]

§ 37. THE GREAT CALVINISTIC DIVINES AGAINST THE ARMINIANS.

The great masters in polemic not only grant that Calvinism held the damnation of infants, but strive to overwhelm and defeat Arminianism for not holding the doctrine.

CLOPPENBURGH: "This dispute has drawn into the question in regard to *infants dying in infancy*; although the Remonstrants themselves do not dare to put into heaven the infants born outside the covenant of grace, of heathen and unbelieving parents, nor to admit them to the communion of grace and glory: because the Apostle too clearly pronounces that they are 'unclean' children. 1 Cor. vii. 14."[145]

"Election embraces all the non reprobates, whether adults or infants: and it is an *impious exception* of the Remonstrants, who exempt the *infants* of the heathen from being subjects of reprobation * * * and prefer to put on an equality the *infants* of unbelieving heathen and of believing Christians."[146] "The nature of a gracious covenant is destroyed, when the infants of the heathen are put upon an equality with the infants of faithful Christians. They (the Remonstrants) themselves admit that the infants of heathen are left by God in a condition of nature, deprived of the good of

---

[143] 57, 6.
[144] Mastricht: Theor. Pract. Theol. Trajecti ad Rhen. 1725, p. 1069. Walch Bibl. Theol. Select. I. 428; II. 549, 550.
[145] Exerc. Sup. Loc. Comm. Theolog. Franck, 1653. De. Elec. grat. 1, § 24.
[146] Do. Locus de electione. Disputat. II.

grace and glory, to be condemned, at least to that eternal death which they define as the 'penalty of loss (*pœna damni*).'"

Here, as in other cases, Calvinism asserts a positive damnation of eternal pain for heathen infants, over against the modified and negative loss which Arminianism conceded.

THE DEAF AND DUMB AND INSANE. —But the ingenuity of these terrible old logicians has not exhausted itself, with the mystery which puts the immensely larger part of infants into the ranks of the reprobate and damned. They go to a hapless part of the race, whose condition even beyond that of infants touches the heart with the saddest pathos. Cloppenburg[147] further makes the charge against the Remonstrants:

"They also exempt *without exception*, all *deaf and dumb persons*, and the *insane*. (*Surdos atque Amentes*).

"For experience shows a distinction between one class of the deaf and dumb, who by signs and pious works manifest (*spirant*) an inward devotion, and another class, in whom sin reveals itself, reigning through the works of the flesh. * * These latter we believe are left dead in sins, under just damnation, through the law of nature."

It is well for the reader to recall the fact that when Cloppenburgh wrote, the possibility of reaching those born deaf, with the Word, was almost unknown. A few isolated attempts had succeeded in the long ages, but their success was regarded as miraculous, or treated as a fable, and whether as miracle or fable, soon forgotten. Jerome Cardan (1501—1576) had asserted the *possibility* of teaching the deaf and dumb. To Pedro Ponce, a Benedictine monk of Spain, belongs the honor

---

[147] Locus de Electione. Disputat. II.

of first attempting to actualize the possibility; to Juan Paulo Boret, another monk of the same order, belongs the honor of publishing the first book (1620) on the subject. Cloppenburgh's argument (1592—1652) implies that he knew nothing of this possibility.

Of the idiotic, insane, and mad, he says, "a distinction is to be made. There are those whom an evil conscience and reprobate mind, by God's just judgment, drives to madness, like mad dogs (*ut canes rabiosos*); who, unless God heals them, cannot be counted with the non-reprobate?"

MOLINÆUS AGAINST THE ARMINIANS.—PETER MOLINÆUS (Dumoulin) 1568—1658, was one of the greatest divines of the French Calvinistie Church, and was deputed to attend the Synod of Dort. The prohibition of Louis XIII. prevented his attendance, but did not prevent his promulgating and defending the decrees of the Synod, and obtaining for them the sanction of the National Synods of Calvinistic France. In the theological chair at Sedan, he was the great opponent of Amyraud and the other professors of Saumur, who were charged with a kind of Semi-Arminianism. He has been regarded as "one of the greatest writers and the first polemic of his age." In his Dissection of Arminianism,[148] he opens with a defense of God's dealings with man, thoroughly characteristic of old Calvinism.

"If any one were to crush an ant with his foot, no one could charge him with injustice, though the ant never offended him, though he did not give life to the ant, though the ant belonged to another, and no restitution could be made, and though between the ant and man the inequality is not infinite, but a certain and finite proportion."

In all these aspects, he argues, the case is

---

[148] Anatome Arminianismi. Lugduni Batav. 1621, 4to, p. 2.

stronger for God, "if He should harden sinful men whom He might save." "The offspring of the pious and faithful are born with the infection of original sin."[149] "As the eggs of the asp are deservedly crushed, and serpents just born are deservedly killed, though they have not yet poisoned any one with their bite, so infants are justly obnoxious to penalties."[150] Molinæus answers the Arminian position that Christ by His death obtained reconciliation for all, by objecting that it would then follow "that all infants born outside of the covenant are reconciled, and have their sins forgiven, and that hence no greater blessing could be conferred on them than the merciful cruelty of cutting their throats in their cradles, (*quam si quis eos clementi crudelitate in cunis jugulaverit*)." [151] Molinæus' suggestion holds with equal force against Dr. Hodge's view that all dying infants are saved. The two together would imply that any man can make the election of an infant sure in the dreadful manner suggested in the bloody age in which Molinæus lived.

"*To him, whom God hates from the womb*, He does not give sufficient and saving grave. Hence there are those whom God rejects with a spiritual rejection, before they have done anything of good or evil. He does not therefore give them sufficient means to faith and salvation, for this cannot be harmonized with hatred." [152]

The same views of infant reprobation are pressed over against the Arminians, by Molinæus[153] in other places.

---

[149] Do., p. 36.
[150] P. 48.
[151] P. 181.
[152] Do., 289.
[153] Thesaurus Sedanensis Genevæ, 1661. 2 Vols. 4to, I. 197.

BURMANN AGAINST THE ARMINIANS.

BURMANN.[154] — "The Remonstrants do evilly, who, though they do not *dare*, on account of 1 Cor. vii. 14, *to put them in heaven*, yet acknowledge no *reprobation of them*, * * but assign them rather a middle state and penalty of loss; as also other, both of the ancients and moderns, *grant heaven to them, in the face of* 1 Cor. vii. 14, and Rom. v. 14."

GUERTLER, AGAINST THE ARMINIANS.

GUERTLER (1654-1711) in arguing against the Arminians, says:

"Death comes even unto infants; *for without reason*, and *contrary* to *Paul's decision*, Episcopius exempts from the number of *those who are to be punished*, INFANTS and IDIOTS (*infantes et fatuos*)."[155]

That our readers may clearly see what it is that is condemned, we will quote the passage to which Guertler refers.

EPISCOPIUS: "The Scripture represents that misery (of death or damnation and sin) as universal, so as to involve the whole human race, that is all men and every man, to wit, in whom that misery can have just place as penalty. *Infants* therefore, as such, as also *idiots* (*fatuos*), the *insane*, the *mad* or *those destitute of the use of reason and free will* we are unwilling to comprehend in that number... They are liberated from that death by special Divine grace."[156]

GUERTLER has been explicit enough, but he makes assurance doubly sure, by proceeding in the next paragraph to say:

"By 'death' is understood, death, temporal and

---

[154] Synop. Theolog. Gencv. 1678, I. 256. £
[155] Institut. Theolog. Amstelod. 1694, pp. 188, 189.
[156] Institut.Theolog.Lib.IV. Sect. V. ch. I. Opera Amstelod. 1650, p. 401.

death eternal; and this latter is the unceasing (*perpetuus*) sense of dire tortures (*dirorum cruciatum*), inevitable to those who see not the face of God, so that the Scholastics, following Lombard, wrongly teach that *infants*, on account of sin, *pay the debt of loss only*, not of sense." The sentence of LOMBARD, which Guertler cites, is as follows: "Not, therefore, for the actual sins of their own parents, nor even for the actual sins of the first parent, but for original (sin) which is derived from the parents, infants will be damned; hence they will not endure the penalty, material fire, or that of the worm of conscience, but will be deprived forever of the vision of God."[157] This mitigation Guertler rejects, and closes the paragraph following, with the decisive words: "God hath ordained (Statuit), that we should be born corrupt, or that we should sin, because Adam hath sinned, and wills that we should die, because we sin."[158]

§38. THE ARMINIANS AGAINST THE CALVINISTS.

The Arminian defenses constantly urge against the Calvinists their doctrine of infant reprobation. It is one, they say, of which Calvinists make no secret, so far as the children of the non-elect, pagan or Christian, are concerned, and which the candid allow involves that some children even of the elect are lost.

EPISCOPIUS. — "Those who believe that absolute election and absolute reprobation pertain to infants dying in infancy, whether they be Gentiles or children of those who are in the covenant—to them the uncertainty (whether they shall grieve or rejoice over the death of their children) is very mournful, for the fear of reprobation far outweighs the hope of election,

---

[157] Lombard, Sentat. L. II. Dort. 33, 1, E.
[158] See also Guertler do. do., p. 202, and the citations he gives from the Remonstrant's Confessions.

since the number of the reprobate is far greater than that of the elect: hence it is clear that an unutterable grief may readily arise from such a death."[159]

GROTIUS shows that in certain aspects the Calvinists departed as completely from the "Catholic faith," in regard to infants, as the Pelagians did in others. If the Calvinists did not hold, with Augustine, that unbaptized infants are lost, neither did they hold, as Augustine did most tenaciously, that all baptized infants are certainly saved. He states the Calvinistic doctrine thus: "That some infants, dying in infancy, and who, as children of believers and baptized, are delivered to the torments of hell on account of original sin."[160]

"Calvin says that of those who have rested on the breasts of the same Christian mother some are borne to heaven, others thrust down to hell, without respect to their having or failing to have Baptism: to wit, by virtue of that decree, by which God hath decreed, not by permitting only, but also by willing, that Adam should necessarily fall, and that so many nations, with their infant children, should through that fall be brought to eternal death without remedy. When Calvin himself calls this decree 'fearful' (*horribile*), he gives it too soft a name (*minus quam res est dixit*)"[161]

LIMBORCH (d. 1712).—"The Contra-remonstrants (the Calvinists) teach that original sin merits the eternal punishment of sense, or the eternal torments of the fire of hell, so that many infants dying in infancy are to be tortured forever in the fire of hell. Thus in common (*communiter*) the Contra-remonstrant divines teach concerning the children of unbelievers who die in infancy. As regards the children of believers they do not openly set forth their judgment. Some say in

---

[159] Responsio ad LXIV. Quaest. 38.
[160] Disquisitio de dogmnt. Pelagian. Opera, Londini, 1689, IV. 376.
[161] Rivet. Apologet. Discuss. Opera, IV. 684.

express words, that the distinction of election and reprobation exists in their case also, and, therefore, some children of believers, dying in infancy, are to be cast into hell. Such is the view of Parieus, Zanchius, Perkins, and Donteklok. Arthur Hildersham, also on Psalm I. Lect. 55, says: "It is clear that God hath declared His wrath against the sins of infants by pursuing with His hatred *not their sins only, but also their persons,* (*non tantum ... ipsorum peccata sed et personas,*) Rom. ix. 11, 13, nor merely by inflicting on them corporeal penalties, but also by casting them into hell. And to put beyond all doubt that he is speaking of the children of believers, in speaking, on Rom. ix., of the children of believers, he says: 'It is a damnable error that all who die in infancy shall certainly obtain the heavenly heritage; on the contrary, he (Paul) decides that *many infants are vessels of wrath and firebrands* of hell (*titiones inferni*).' Others, not daring to confess this openly, cover the hideousness (*fœditatem*) of their position with ambiguous words, by saying that we, in accordance with God's revealed will, expressed in this formula of the divine covenant, and in accordance with the judgment of charity, ought to regard as elect all the children of believers, as embraced in the same covenant with their parents. But as they hold that the secret will of God is often contrary to His revealed will, and that we are obliged sometimes to believe, according to the revealed will, what is false according to the secret will: and as many according to the judgment of charity are to be esteemed elect, who are in fact not elect, it is evident that there is here no certitude of faith, and that they have devised this, only to disguise their opinion, whose hideousness they desire, as far as they can, to conceal."[162]

---

[162] Theologia Christiana. Amsterdam, 1700. Lib. III. Ch. V. iii. p. 187.

§ 39. THE WESTMINSTER ASSEMBLY. (1643—45.)

But perhaps the Westminster Assembly, which embraced in its Confession the particular type of Calvinism to which Dr. Hodge is bound, and of which he is, indisputably, one of the noblest representatives—perhaps this Assembly may have been marked by special mildness—and mitigating its logic by its gentleness, may have qualified the rigor of the older view? Such a supposition could only be made in ignorance and in irony. The Calvinism of the Westminster Assembly was in no respect milder than that of the Synod of Dort. Its prolocutor, Dr. Twiss, Dr. Thomas Goodwin, one of its very greatest members, and others, were of the extremest Supralapsarian school, that school of which distinguished Calvinists of a milder type have spoken so severely. Thomas Case, one of its most esteemed members, was so zealous for religion, as he understood it, that in a sermon before the Court Martial, 1644, he said: "Noble sirs, imitate God, and be merciful to none that have sinned of malicious wickedness," meaning the Royalists.[163]

Dr. Philip Schaff says of the Westminster Assembly: "The Presbyterians were opponents of all tolerance, and were as urgent for a general uniformity as the Episcopalians had been under Elizabeth and Charles II. They regarded freedom of conscience and tolerance as culpable indifference and treason toward revealed truth."[164] The writings of the Westminster divines, and of all the earlier school which followed in their footsteps, sustain the sense we have given to the Westminster Confession in regard to infant damnation. These writings are in English and easy of access, and we need not therefore swell our testimonies with them. The meaning of a Confession when it is made, remains

---

[163] Neal's History of the Puritans, ii. 301.
[164] Hertzog: Art. Westminster Synode, Vol. XVIII. 56.

its meaning forever—and hence the vital importance of the earliest writers, the authors of Confessions, and the original interpreters, expounders, and defenders of them. It is the meaning these writers put upon the Calvinistic Confessions, not one imagined by ourselves, which we have given them; and on the express language of the Confessions, and of these witnesses, we rest our case.

§ 40. ATTEMPTS AT MITIGATION OF THE CALVINISTIC DOCTRINE OF INFANT DAMNATION.

Though Calvinists have regarded the doctrine of infant damnation as involved in the logic of the case, they have not been able to repress the promptings of our common humanity, which Christianity does not repress, but intensifies. The evidence of this human feeling is also the evidence of the fixedness of the doctrine of infant damnation in the system. The attempts to mitigate its horrors, show that they could not abandon the doctrine itself. The confession of this feeling of a need of mitigation shows itself in various ways.

1. In some by a virtual acknowledgment of the principle of the Limbus Infantum. Fighting the name, and part of the definition given by the Church of Rome, many of the Calvinists have granted, in substance, the thing.

MARTYR.[165] — "Young infants must be punished (in hell-fire). But it is credible they shall be the *easier punished*."

CHAMIER.[166] — "Infants guilty of original sin only, in very deed suffer the eternal fire, prepared for the devil and his angels. Although the *opinion* of

---

[165] Common Places, I. 234.
[166] Panstrat. Cathol. Contract. Spanheim, 795.

Augustine is not *improbable*, that *their pains are the mildest.*"

MOLINÆUS.[167] — "Here," ("of the infants of unbelievers") "nevertheless language should he sober. We piously presume that a good God acts clemently, with those little souls, (animulis), and that *their punishment is far lighter* than the punishment of those who polluted by their proper, and personal sins, die without the grace of Christ."

STAPFER[168]— "They will be damned: but there are *various grades* of the sense of that penalty and of damnation, so that the penalty of infants, and the share of it will be the *least,* and therefore differs much from that of the devil, and of adults voluntarily persevering in their sins; so that here also God will be found just in His ways."

§ 41. INFANT ANNIHILATION.

2. DR. WATTS could, as a Calvinist, find no escape from the doctrine that there are reprobate infants, and that they ofttimes die in infancy. He could not as a Calvinist receive the doctrine of a mitigated punishment of them. In pure desperation, in the struggle between the necessities of his system, and his instincts as a human creature, he embraces the theory that *reprobate infants, are probably annihilated* at death:

"The salvation of *all* children ... has *no countenance* from the Bible, ... *no foundation in reason.* The Scripture brings down the infants of wicked parents to the grave, and leaves them there, and so do I. The Scripture has not provided any resurrection for them, neither can I do it."[169]

---

[167] Thesaurus. Disputat. Theolog. in Sedan. Acad. I. 212.
[168] Instit. Theol. Polem. IV., 518.
[169] Ruin and Recovery of Mankind, Quest. XVI.

§ 42. MEDIATING TENDENCY.

3. In the period which has followed the lapse of nearly two centuries, some of the Calvinistic divines begin to show a hesitation on the doctrine, a disposition to qualify it. Especially is this the case with the mediating divines on the Continent who were anxious for union with the Lutheran Church. But in no case do these writers pretend to sustain their views by citations from the Calvinistic authorities or the standard Calvinistic divines. In this general school we place DR. HODGE, and it is true of him as of the others, that he does not attempt by a solitary citation from a Calvinistic Confession, or a standard Calvinistic divine, to maintain his position that all who die in infancy are certainly saved.

DR. HODGE'S position, indeed, in 1860, as given in a quotation in the "Outlines of Theology,"[170] seemed to involve what we suppose to be the correct view of the meaning of the Confession. In epitomizing the doctrine of the Confession he says: "By the right use of this ordinance the grace promised is ... conferred by the Holy Spirit to such (whether of age or *infants*) *as that grace belongeth unto.* That baptism does not in all cases secure the blessings of the covenant... That their blessings *depend* upon two things: (1) the right use ...; (2) the *secret purpose of God.*" In seeming, therefore, now to deny that the purpose of God in regard to dying infants is secret, he increases our surprise that he does not vindicate or at least explain an apparent change of opinion.

§ 43. LUTHERANIZING TENDENCY.

4. Some of the Reformed divines, divines of the "greatest renown," and "of the first order," as WITSIUS[171]

---

[170] 501, 502.
[171] Miscellan. Sacr. II. 618.

calls them, have shown a strong leaning to views, in conflict with their Calvinism, and in various degrees, in approximation to the Lutheran doctrine. They have maintained that regeneration and justification, are not only signified but are *imparted* in Baptism, either to *all* infants, or at least to the elect. The more logical Calvinism has been completely anti-Augustinian in regard to the *objective force of Baptism*. This latter doctrine was so thoroughly inwrought from the beginning into the faith and life of the Church, that both AUGUSTINE and PELAGIUS, with whose extremes it stood in about equal conflict, were obliged to acknowledge it, to accept it as an immovable fact, with which their systems *must*, in some way, be harmonized. The objective force of Baptism is irreconcilable on the one side with the absolute decree of Augustine, which logically demands that sacraments are meant for and shall have validity only for the elect; it is irreconcilable on the other with the Pelagian denial of the corruption of human nature, and of an infant's need of regeneration.

AUGUSTINE nevertheless was compelled by the fixed faith of the Church to acknowledge that all baptized infants are justified, and that consequently original sin is remitted to them in Baptism—and so far the ancient Augustinian school was a unit. It divided, however, on another point. Augustine held that this pardon was revocable—God could take it back, and in the case of the *reprobate* infallibly did take it back. PROSPER maintained, on the contrary, that the forgiveness of original sin in Baptism was irrevocable, and that if any one after Baptism fell from Christ and grace, and was lost, he was condemned for his *actual* sins only: his original sin remaining, still and forever, pardoned.

Many of the greatest of the Reformed divines have been overwhelmed with what they grant is on this point—the objective force of Baptism—the faith of all the fathers and of the entire Christian Church through all the ages before the rise of Calvinism.[172]

LE BLANC maintains that: "Sacraments not only seal grace received, but are also means of receiving grace, and are signs of a certain grace present, which is conferred and communicated with them."[173]

JURIEU, (1637-1713) is confessedly one of the greatest names in the history of Calvinism and of the Christian Church. His views are thus epitomized by Witsius.* Jurieu maintains that: "God ordinarily confers His grace at the time in which He represents it: the elect infants of those in covenant are, previous to their Baptism, children of wrath; they are not loved by God with the love of complacency till they are baptized and washed from those stains, with which we are all born; by Baptism the liability arising from original sin is so removed, that none who are baptized are condemned on account of original sin: that infants legitimately baptized and dying in infancy are certainly saved, and that this baptism is an indubitable proof of their election: that baptism is as necessary to salvation as food to life, or medicine to healing: that God can and does save some infants without baptism—but this is done in an extraordinary way."

To the names of the defenders of these views among the Reformed are to be added the names of PAREUS, BARON, FORBES, DAVENANT, (delegate from the King of England, at Dort, afterwards Bishop) and WARD, Professor at Cambridge, (also a delegate at Dort), All of these divines were of the Lutheranizing type within the Reformed Churches, and WITSIUS shows at large that their views are wholly irreconcilable with Calvinism.[174]

---

[172] Witsius, Miscellan. II. 640.
[173] Quoted by Witsius. Miscell. Sac. II. 652.
[174] Witsius, Miscell. II. 618.

§ 44. Reformed Liturgies.

5. Such, however, has been the force of testimony on the point that regeneration is ordinarily conferred at the time of Baptism, that this fact has been recognized not only, as we have seen, by great divines, but in defiance of its inconsistency with the system, in more than one of the Reformed Liturgies and other official documents.

In LEO JUDA'S and ZWINGLI'S Form of 1523, the Priest after dipping the child in the water, says: "God ... who hath begotten thee again from on high, and hath forgiven thee all thy sins, anoint thee, &c."[175]

In the Form for the ministration of Baptism in the CHURCH OF ENGLAND, after the Baptism the Priest says: "Seeing ... that this child *is* regenerate ... we yield Thee hearty thanks that it hath pleased Thee to regenerate this infant with Thy Holy Spirit." Burnet argues that this part of the Book of Common Prayer is irreconcilable with Calvinism, and he is right.

THE CHURCH OF ENGLAND, in her form of Baptism, as distinctly affirms the doctrine of baptismal regeneration, as does any part of Christendom. The originals of her form of Baptism, whether she draws them from the Lutheran Church, or from the old Church of the West, mean baptismal regeneration beyond dispute, and she took the forms because they have this meaning.

No part of what has been claimed as belonging to the Reformed Church, as early and as completely as she, has delivered itself from the whole disposition to consign infants to damnation, though within the Church the party of high Calvinists, more faithful to Calvinism than to the general spirit of the Church of England, teach, in accordance with their system the doctrine of infant damnation. USSHER, for example, does

---

[175] Daniel's Codex Liturgio. III., 111.

it in the strongest terms.

If Calvinism be the doctrine of the Church of England, the conflict is not solely between the Articles and the Common Prayer, but between the Articles themselves. This conflict is more marked in the Latin original of the Articles than in the English version. In the Second Article of the Thirty-nine, the Church of England literally transfers the very words of the Augsburg Confession (Art. III.) that "Christ died, not only for *original sin*, but for *all* the actual sins of *men*." That seems to teach universal atonement. She teaches (in Art. XVI.) that "after we have received the Holy Spirit we may depart from grace given." That is hardly final perseverance. She says in Art. XXV. transferring verbatim part of Aug. Conf., Art. XIII., "that sacraments are *efficacious* signs of grace, *through which* God operates on us," and "quickens," that is, *excites* (Lat. excitat) "*faith*, as well as *confirms* it." That is not the Calvinistic doctrine which separates the efficacy from the signs, and denies that sacraments originate gracious conditions.

She declares (Art. XXVII.) "that by Baptism as *by an instrument*, they that receive Baptism rightly, are *grafted* (inserted: Lat. inseruntur) *into* the Church." That seems to concede the objective force of the sacrament. She teaches (in Art. XXXI.) "that the offering of Christ once made, is that perfect redemption, propitiation, and satisfaction for *all* the sins, both original and actual, of the *whole world*" —and this seems to be unlimited atonement again. These and other passages are, in their natural and obvious sense, irreconcilable with Calvinism, and have taxed the ingenuity of the Calvinistic expositors to the utmost.

The doctrine of the Church of England has been throughout that "it is certain by God's Word that children, *being baptized*, (if they *depart out of this life in their infancy)* are certainly saved."[176]

To this was added in the Articles of 1536, that children, dying unbaptized, are not saved: "Infants and children dying in their infancy shall undoubtedly be saved thereby, *or else not.*"[177] The *negation is omitted* in all the later statements,— the official statement of the Church of England is, that baptized infants are certainly saved. She nowhere, in any document in present force, asserts in terms that unbaptized infants are certainly lost. All her affirmations as to the certainty of the salvation of all baptized infants have been the objects of steady opposition on the part of decided Calvinists.

In the Rubric of 1662, to the form of Public Baptism, were added the words: "It is certain by God's Word that children which are baptized, dying before they commit actual sin, are undoubtedly saved." The Rubric stands to this day. Baxter, one of the most moderate of Calvinists, declares that if this Rubric were the only thing in the way, it would be sufficient to prevent him and his associates from conforming to the Church, whatever they might suffer for their refusal. He pronounces it a new Article of Faith; a dangerous addition to God's Word; a doctrine unheard of before the last change of the Liturgy. Think of it! The Calvinists of England, represented by one of the most moderate of their number, declaring it a sufficient reason for refusing to conform, that the Church of England does not teach that some baptized infants, dying in infancy, are damned.[178]

The old Liturgy of the Reformed Church of

---

[176] Articles of the Convocation, 1536. Homily on Salvation, 1547. Preface to Confirmation, Book 1549, and to Books of 1552, and the Book of Elizabeth.

[177] Quoted from Wilkins' Concilia, III.;818, in Bulley's Tabular View, (1842) 254.

[178] Baxter: English Non-conformity, C. LX. Quoted in Bingham: Apology of the French Church, L. iii. C, 18.

France has also been claimed as supporting their views, by the Reformed divines, who maintain that regeneration is ordinarily conferred on infants in the moment of Baptism—not before.[179]

§ 45. CONCLUSION.

We have endeavored frankly to meet what we have considered a virtual challenge to make good our position. We now make, not a challenge, but a request. We request any and all defenders of Calvinism to produce a solitary Calvinistic standard or divine, from the First Helvetic Confession to the Westminster Confession, or from Calvin to Twiss, the Prolocutor of the Westminster Assembly, in which, or by whom, it is asserted or implied that all who die in infancy are certainly saved.

The discussion into which we have here entered was not one of our own seeking. Calvinism itself has loved to raise the question as to this position of its own view, and the old churchly doctrine of Baptismal Regeneration to the doctrine of Infant Salvation. It was a charge made by Dr. A. A. HODGE,[180] now of Alleghany Seminary, against the Lutheran views, which led us to the argument finally embodied in our Conservative Reformation—the argument designed to show that the doctrine of Baptism, as the ordinary channel of Regeneration, places infant salvation on the securest ground. In connection with this argument occur our words which Dr. CHARLES HODGE thinks are not sustained by the Confessions and history of Calvinism.

If the historical argument we offer in vindication of our interpretation does no more than satisfy the revered author of the Systematic Theology,

---

[179] Witsius. Miscell. Exercertat. XIX. Vol. II. 640.
[180] Outlines of Theology, 1860. P. 502.

that our interpretation was not wantonly or hastily assumed, we shall feel that we have not written in vain. The facts we have drawn together, we present purely in the interests of truth, with no personal animosity to Calvinism, still less to its representatives. We know how many noble men, and noble works have been associated in the past and are associated in the present with Calvinism. Many of the dearest, holiest and most treasured ties of our life are those which unite us to members and ministers within its various communions. For its services and sacrifices in behalf of our common Christianity we love and revere it, and this love and reverence is not the mystery of this Review, but very largely the occasion of it.

BAPTISM:
THE DOCTRINE SET FORTH IN
HOLY SCRIPTURE,
AND TAUGHT IN THE
EVANGELICAL LUTHERAN CHURCH.

BY CHARLES P. KRAUTH, D. D.

Norton Professor of Theology in the Theological Seminary of the Evangelical Lutheran Church, at Philadelphia.

GETTYSBURG:

J. E. WIBLE, PRINTER, NORTH-EAST CORNER OF THE DIAMOND.

1866.

Baptism

OUR Lord, in the course of his earthly ministry, authorized his disciples to baptize, (John 4:1, 2) and previous to his ascension, commanded them to make disciples of all the Rations, by baptizing them in the name of the Father, and of the Son, and of the Holy Spirit, (Matt. 28:19.) The rite of Baptism thus enjoined by our Lord, has been the subject of various disputes in the Christian world. It is the object of this article to exhibit the faith of the Evangelical Lutheran Church in regard to the points of dispute.

Over against all who deny the divine institution and perpetuity of Baptism, our Church maintains that "God has instituted it," and that it is obligatory and necessary throughout all time (Aug. Conf., Art. V, AC I.VII,-XIV) so that without it the Church cannot exist in the world.

Serious differences of opinion, however, exist in Christendom, even among those who recognize the perpetuity and obligation of Baptism, as to what is *essential* to Baptism, even as to its outward part. For, while all are agreed that the use of water, and of the Word, are essential, some parts of the Christian world maintain that the essential idea of Baptism, is that of the *total immersion* of the body, insomuch that this *immersion is absolutely necessary,* and *positively demanded by our Lord,* and the application of water in any other way, whatsoever, is no Baptism. THE LUTHERAN CHURCH DOES NOT HOLD that immersion is ESSENTIAL TO BAPTISM.

Luther and the Jewess.

Attempts have, indeed, been made to show that Luther, at least, held the necessity of immersion, and that the Lutheran Church either held it with him, or was inconsistent in rejecting it.

One of the passages most frequently appealed to, in the attempt to implicate Luther, is found in Walch's Edition of his works, X, 2,637. In regard to this, the following are the facts:

1. The passage referred to is from a letter of Luther, written from Coburg, July 9th, 1530, in reply to an Evangelical pastor, Henry Genesius, who had consulted him in regard to the Baptism of a Jewish girl.

It will be noted from the date, that the letter was written a few months after the issue of the Catechisms, in which it is pretended, as we shall see, that he taught the necessity of immersion.

2. The letter given in Walch, is also in the Leipzig edition of Luther, (XXII, 371,) and is not in the original language, but is a translation, and that from a defective copy of the original. The original Latin is given in De Wette's edition of Luther's Briefe, (IV, 8,) and contains a most important part of a sentence which is not found in the German translation. The letter in Walch cannot, therefore, be cited in evidence, for it is neither the original, nor a reliable translation of it.

3. The whole letter shows that the main point of inquiry was not as to whether the girl should be baptized in this or that mode, but what precautions decency demanded during the baptism, provided it were done by immersion.

4. Luther says, "It WOULD PLEASE me, therefore, that she should *   * modestly have the water POURED UPON HER, *(Mihi placeret, ut,   *   * verecunde perfunderetur)* or, if she sit in the water up to her neck, that her head should be immersed with a trine immersion," *(Caput   ejus   trina   immersione immergeretur.)*

5. An *immersionist* is one who contends that Baptism *must* be administered by immersion. The

passage quoted is decisive that Luther did not think Baptism *must* be so administered. He represents it as pleasing to him, best of all, that the girl should have the water applied to her by pouring, or that, if she were immersed, greater precautions, for the sake of decency, should be observed, than were usual in the Church of Rome. It is demonstrated by this very letter, that LUTHER WAS NOT AN IMMERSIONIST.

6. In suggesting the two modes of Baptism, Luther was simply following the Ritual of the Romish Church. In the Romish Ritual the direction is: "Baptism may be performed either by pouring, immersion, or sprinkling; but either the first or second mode, which are most in use, shall be retained, according as it has been the usage of the Churches to employ the one or the other, so that either THE HEAD OF THE PERSON to be baptized shall have a trine ablution—that is, either the water shall be POURED UPON IT, *(perfundatum*—Luther quotes the very word,) or the HEAD shall be immersed, *(ut trina ablutione caput immergatur)*—Luther again quotes almost verbatim.

In the Romish Ritual, furthermore, for the baptism of adults, it is said, "But in the Churches where Baptism is performed by immersion, either of the *entire body*, or of the head only, the priest shall baptize by thrice immersing *the person*, or his head," *(illum vel caput ejus.)* Luther directed, in case the Jewess were immersed at all, that the officiating minister should immerse her head only. She was to seat herself in the bath, and the only religious immersion was not that of her whole body, (as Rome permits, and the Baptists, if consistent, would prescribe); but of her *head* only, *(ut caput ejus immergeretur.)* Luther, so far as he allowed of immersion at all, was not as much of an immersionist as the Ritual of Rome might have made him, for he does not hint at the immersion of the *whole body* of the Jewess by the minister. An immersionist contends that the whole body must be submerged by the officiating minister; not indeed that he is to lift the whole body and plunge it in, but the. whole immersion is to be so conducted as to be clearly his official work, the person being led by him into the water, and the immersion completed by his bending the body and thus bringing beneath the surface what was up to that time uncovered. Luther preferred, if there was to be an immersion, that the *head* only, not the *body*, should be immersed by the minister, (not *illum sed caput ejus.*) Even to the extent, therefore, to which he allowed immersion, *Luther was no immersionist.*

7. If Luther could be proved by this letter to be an immersionist, it would be demonstrated that he derived his view from the Romish Church, and held it in common with her. In like manner, the Church of England, the Episcopal Churches of Scotland and of the United States, and the Methodist Churches, would be carried over to the ranks of immersionists, for they allow the different modes. But these Churches are confessedly not immersionist; therefore, *Luther was no immersionist.*

8. Whatever Luther's personal preferences may have been as to mode, he never even *doubted* the validity of Baptism by pouring. But immersionists do not merely doubt it, they absolutely deny it; therefore, *Luther was no immersionist.*

9. An immersionist is one who makes his particular mode of Baptism a term of Church communion, and an article of faith. Luther was in a Church which did not prescribe immersion as necessary—never made it an article of faith; therefore, *Luther was no immersionist.*

10. Finally, the letter of Luther shows that he *preferred pouring.* He says expressly that it would please him that the water should be poured upon her, and gives this the first place; and his directions in

regard to the immersion, are given only in the supposition that that mode might be decided upon—"if she sit, &c, her head shall be immersed," &c, *si sedens.*

Whatever, therefore, may be the difference between the doctrine of the necessity of immersion, and the "doctrine of immersion," we feel safe in affirming that Luther held neither.

Luther's Catechisms.

From Luther's Larger Catechism, by confounding the very plain distinction between allowance, or preference of a mode, and a belief in its necessity, the evidence has been drawn that our Confessions teach the Baptist doctrine of immersion.

Yet this very Catechism, in express terms, repudiates any such doctrine, and acknowledges, in the most decisive manner, what the Baptist doctrine denies—the validity of other modes than immersion. Mark these two sentences from the Larger Catechism: "Baptism is not our work, but God's. For thou must distinguish between the Baptism which God gives, and that which the keeper of a bath-house gives. But God's work, to be saving, does not exclude faith, but demands it, for without faith it cannot be grasped. For in the mere fact that *thou hast had water poured on thee,* thou hast not so received Baptism as to be useful to thee; but it profits thee when thou art baptized with the design of obeying God's command and institution, and in God's name of receiving in the water the salvation promised. This neither the hand nor the body can effect, but the heart must believe."[181] In these words there is an express recognition of pouring or sprinkling, (for the word used by Luther covers both, but excludes immersion,) as modes of Baptism.

---

[181] Catech. Maj. Müller, 490, 36, *das Wasser über dich giessen.* The Latin is, "*aqua perfundi*"

But there is another passage yet more decisive, if possible. "We must look upon our Baptism, and so use it, as to strengthen and comfort us, whenever we are grieved by sins and conscience. We should say: I am baptized, therefore, the promise of salvation is given me for soul and body. For to this end *these two things are done in* Baptism, that the body which can only receive the water, *is wet by pouring,* and that, in addition, the word is spoken that the soul may receive it."[182] Here not only is the recognition of pouring (or sprinkling) explicit, but if the words were not compared with other expressions of Luther, it might be argued, that he and our symbols went to the opposite extreme from that charged upon them, and instead of teaching that immersion is necessary, denied its validity. So far, then, is the charge from being verified, that we are authorized to make directly the opposite statement. Luther and our Confessions repudiate, utterly, the Baptist doctrine of the *necessity* of immersion.

In the *original* of the Smaller Catechism there is not a word about immersion in a passage sometimes referred to. It is simply, "What signifies this *Water*-Baptism?" (Wasser-Taüffen.) "Immersion" is but a translation of a translation. The same is the case with the Smalcald Articles. The original reads, "Baptism is none other thing than God's word *in the water, (im wasser,)*" and not a word about immersion. We do not rule these translations out because they at all sustain the allegation. Fairly interpreted, they do not; but we acknowledge the obvious rule accepted in such cases— that the originals of documents, and not translations of them, are the proper subjects of appeal.

A translation can carry no authority, except as it correctly exhibits the sense of the original. Even the

---

[182] Do. 492. German: „*Der Leib begossen wird"* Latin: „*Corpus aqua perfundatur."*

general endorsement of a translation as correct by the author of the original, is not decisive, on a minute point which he may have overlooked, or have thought a matter of very little importance. A clergyman of our Church translated the commentary of an eminent German theologian, and received from him a warm letter of thanks, strongly endorsing the accuracy of the translation. Yet, not only in a possible deviation of the translation from the original, but in any matter of doubt, however slight, the original alone would be the source of appeal. As the Lutheran Church accepts Luther's version of the Bible, subject to correction by the original, so does she accept any translation of her symbols, however excellent, subject to correction by the original.

But, even if the principle were not otherwise clear, the facts connected with the translation of the different parts of the Symbolical Books, would be decisive on this point. The translation of the Smalcald Articles, made in 1541, by Generanus, a young Danish student of Theology, at Wittemberg, and who was an intimate friend of Luther, was confessedly admirable, pithy, and Luther-like, yet the translation which appeared in the Book of Concord, in 1580, was an *entirely new one,* very inferior to the old one, and this, after undergoing two sets of changes, is the one now ordinarily found in the Latin editions of the Symbol.

This is one of the translations to which appeal is made, in the face of the original, and language is used which leaves the reader under the impressien that these articles were translated under Luther's eye, and the translation approved by him.

The German translation of the Apology, found in the *Uditio Princeps* of the German Concordia, and in most other editions, adds some things which are not in the Latin, and omits some things which are there. Which is the authority, Melanchthon's Latin, or Jonas'

German, if a dispute arise as to the meaning of the Apology?

3. The Larger Catechism was first translated by Lonicer, faithfully, and into good Latin. The second translation was made by Opsopasus, and this was *changed* in various respects by Selnecker, and thus changed, was introduced into the Book of Concord.

4. The Smaller Catechism was first rendered into Latin by an unknown hand, then by Sauermann. "This translation *seems* to have been introduced into the Concordien-buch, *but with changes,*" says Köllner.

The principle involved, which no honest scholar would try to weaken, is well stated by Walch, in these words :[183] "It is by all means proper to know what was the *original language* of each of our Symbolical Books, since it is manifest, that from *that, not from translations,* we are to judge of the genuine and true meaning of any book. What they teach, we ought to see, not in versions, but in the original language itself, especially where the matter or meaning seems involved in some doubt. Versions do not always agree entirely with the writings as their authors composed them; as the facts themselves show is the case in our Symbolical Books also."

The allusions of Luther to the outward mode are never found in his *definition* of Baptism. His allusions to immersion come, in every case, long after he has defined Baptism. His *definition* of Baptism, in the Smalcald Articles, is: "Baptism is none other thing than the word of God in the water, enjoined by his institution." His *definition* of Baptism in the Larger Catechism, is thus: "Learn thou, when asked, What *is* Baptism? to reply, It is not mere water, but a water embraced in God's word and command." It is a mere illusion of the devil when our New Spirits of the day

---

[183] *introd. in Lib., Symbol, 61

ask, "How can a *handful of water* help the soul?" And then comes his powerful vindication of this "handful of water" in its connection with the word. In the Smaller Catechism, to the question, What is Baptism? the reply is, "Baptism is not mere water, but that water which is comprehended in God's command, and bound up with God's word." Nowhere does any Symbol of our Church say that Baptism *is* immersion, or even allude to immersion when it speaks of that which constitutes Baptism.

That the word "begiessen," by which Luther indicates one of the modes of Baptism, can only indicate pouring or sprinkling, and by no possibility immersion, every one even moderately acquainted with German, very well knows. The proper meaning of *begiessen,* as given by Adelung, is, *"Durch Giessen nass machen,"* i. e., to wet by pouring or dropping. Campe's definition is, *"Durch Darangiessen einer Flüssigkeit nass machen,"* i. e., to wet by the pouring on of a fluid. Frisch defines it: *Perfundi, affundendo madefacere,"* i. e., to pour over, to wet by pouring upon. The Grimms define it by, *"Perfundere,"* to pour over. When followed by *"mit,"* governing a noun, the *"mit"* is always to be translated *"with," "mit wasser begiessen,"* to wet by pouring the water. When followed by "*auf,*" the *"auf"* means "upon." When Adler gives "moisten," "bathe," "soak," and similar words as an equivalent, it is in such phrases as, "to bathe or moisten *(begiessen)* the hand with tears." You may use *"begiessen,"* when the hand is bathed by the tears which pour or drop upon it; but if the hand were bathed by immersing it in water, a German would no more use *"begiessen"* to designate that act than we would use "pour." We affirm what every German scholar knows, that with any allusion, direct or indirect, to the mode in which a liquid can be brought into contact with an object, *"begiessen"* never means, and never can mean, either in whole or inclusively, "to immerse." It is so remote from it as to be antithetical to it, and is the very word used over against the terms for immersion, when it is desirable distinctly to state that Baptism is not to be performed in that way. But if *"begiessen"* could ever mean to immerse, or include that idea, we shall demonstrate specially that it has not that force in Luther's German.

Luther uses the word *giessen* upwards of fifty times in his translation of the Bible, and invariably in the primary sense of pour. The word *"begiessen"* in which the prefix *"be"* simply gives a transitive character to the *"giessen,"*—as we might say "bepour," he uses five times. Twice he uses it in the Old Testament, to translate "Yah-tzak," which in twenty other passages he translates by *"giessen,"* to pour. The two passages in which *begiessen* is used, are, Gen. 35:14, "Jacob *poured (begoss)* oil thereon,"—hardly, we think, immersed his pillar of stone in oil; Job 38:38, "Who can stay the bottles of heaven, when the dust groweth (Marg: Hebr: is poured, *begossen)* into hardness,"—hardly meaning that the compacting of the mire is made by immersing the ground into the showers. Three times Luther uses *"begiessen"* in the New Testament, 1 Cor. 3:6, 7, 8, "Apollos watered: he that watereth *(begossen, begeusat)*—referring to the sprinkling, or pouring of water on plants. So Luther, also says, "Hatred and wrath are poured over me, *(uber mich begossen,)"* Jena Ed., 5:55.)

We have shown that the general usage of the language does not allow of the interpretation in question. We have shown that, if it did, Luther's German does not. We shall now show, that if both allowed it anywhere, it is most especially not allowable in the Catechism, nor in Luther's use of it anywhere, with reference to Baptism.

Now for *"begiessen,"* in its reference to Baptism by Luther, in the Catechism and elsewhere, can it *include not exclude* immersion? Let us try this.

1. Larger Catechism: *Dass du lässest das Wasser über dich giessen, (quod te aqua perfundi sinis.)* We affirm that these words have, to anyone who knows anything of German, but one possible meaning, and that, like the literal English translation of the words "that thou lettest the water pour over thee," the German cannot mean "thou lettest thyself be dipped into the water."

2. What *mode of* Baptism Luther had in his mind, is clear, furthermore, from the words in immediate connection with those we have quoted, for he says: "This (the work of the heart) the bent hand (Faust[184]) cannot do, nor the body," the connection showing the thought to be this: neither the bent hand of the administrator of Baptism, bent to gather up and pour the water, nor the body of the recipient, can take the place of faith, in securing the blessings of Baptism.

3. This is rendered clear again, from the words "*Was sollt ein hand voll Wassers der Seelen helfen?*" What can a *handful* of water help the soul? This shows that the "handful of water" was connected with a received mode at that time in the Lutheran Churches.

If the sense of *begiessen,* as applied to Baptism, were obscure, (as it is not—no word more clearly excludes immersion) this passage would settle it.

4. But there is abundance more of evidence on this point. In Luther's Ritual for Baptism, the officiating minister "pours the water," *(geusst wasser auf,)* and says: *"Ich taüfe dich.*

5. In the Article of Torgau, the fanatics, who in the Catechism are characterized as asking, "What can the handful of water do," are represented as calling Baptism "miserable water, or pouring," *(Begiessen.)*

---

[184] As in Isaiah, 40:12, "*Wer missel die Wasser mit der Faust*" Eng. Ver.: "Who hath measured the water in the *hollow of his hand?* ".

6. In the letter of July 9th, 1530, "That standing, she should have the water poured upon her, *(perfunderetur)* or sitting, her head should be immersed, *(immergeretur,)*" surely not both the same.

7. In the Wittenberg Liturgy, of 1542, those are spoken of who do "not dip *(tauchen)* the infants in water, nor *(noch)* pour it upon them, *(begiessen.)*"

But Luther says, *the body* is baptized; therefore, of necessity it is urged, by immersion. When St. Paul describes Baptism in the words "having our bodies washed with pure water," he can hardly be said to prove himself an immersionist. Luther's words are: "These two things are done in Baptism, that the body, which is able to receive nothing besides the water, is wet by pouring, and, in addition, the Word is spoken, that the *soul* may embrace it. Body and soul are the two things in Luther's mind, and it is not hard to see that the body does receive what is poured on the head.

But if the criticism of the word "body," stood, it would do no good, for water can be applied to the entire body, by pouring or sprinkling, as was largely, though not universally, the usage in our Church.

Luther, in speaking of the permanence of the Baptismal Covenant, and of the power of returning, by repentance, to its blessings, even after we fall into sin, says: *"Aber mit Wasser ob man sich gleich hundertmal lasset ins Wasser senken, ist doch nicht mehr denn Eine Taufe."* This has been thus translated and annotated: "But no one dares to *'begiessen'* us with water again: for if one should be sunk in water *[ins wasser senken)* a hundred times, it is no more than one Baptism?" Here *senken* is used along with *begiessen,* and to explain it.

But neither the translation, nor interpretation, is accurate. *"Darf"* does not mean "dares." but means "needs," as the Latin has it, *"non est necesse."* The *"ob gleich"* has been dropped, those important words, which the Latin properly renders *"etsi,"* "for *even though* one should be sunk." *"Senken"* is not used to explain *begiessen.* Luther does not mean that to *"pour* upon *with* water" is equivalent to being *"sunk in* water a *hundred* times." The point is this: After the one Baptism, the repentant sinner needs not that water should be poured upon him again. No re-pouring can make a re-baptism. Nay, if he were not merely *poured* upon, but *sunk* into the water, not *once* but a *hundred* times, still, in spite of the quantity of the water, and the manifold repetition of the rite, there would be but one Baptism. There is an ANTITHESIS, not a PARALLEL, between POUR and SINK, and ONCE and a HUNDRED TIMES.

Luther's Translation of the Bible.

Luther's translation of the words connected with Baptism, proves that he was no immersionist.

1. Immersionists say that Baptism should *always* be translated *immersion.* Luther, throughout his translation of the Bible, NEVER translates it *immersion, (untertauchung)* or *dipping, (eintauchung)* or *plunging, (versenkung)* but always, and exclusively, Baptism (*Taufe.)*

2. Immersionists translate *Baptismos* immmersion. Luther translates it either Baptism or washing. Mark 7 :4,— Baptist Version: *Immersion* of cups, &c. Luther: *washing.* Do. 8,—Baptist Version: *immersions;* Luther: *washing.*

3. *a.* Immersionists say that *Baptizo* should always be translated to immerse. Luther *never* translates it by immerse, nor any of its equivalents, but with the exceptions we shall mention in a moment, by *Taufen,* to baptize.

b. Immersionists say, moreover, that *en* following *baptizo,* should be translated *in,* "I immerse you *in* water;" "he shall immerse you *in* the Holy Spirit," &c. Luther translates as does our English version: "I baptize you *with (mit)* water;" "he shall baptize you *with* the Holy Spirit," &c.

c. Luther translates 1 Cor. 15:29, "What shall they do which are baptized *above* the dead," and explains it, (Leipz. Ed. X, 384,) of administering Baptism *"at the graves of the dead"* in token of faith in the resurrection. The words of Luther are: "They are baptized at the graves of the dead, in token that the dead who lay buried there, and *over whom* they were baptized, would rise again. As we also might administer Baptism publicly, in the common church-yard, or burial place." Auslegung, Anno 1534.

Immersionists generally prefer to consider the Baptism here as metaphorical, and immerse the live saints in sorrows.

4. Immersionists say that the *radical* idea of *Baptizo,* in its New Testament use, is not that of *washing.* Luther repeatedly translates it, *to wash.* We will present some of" these translations in contrast: Translation on Immersionist principles: Judith 12:8, "Judith went out and *immersed* herself at a spring near the camp;" Luther: *"and washed* herself in the Water." Ecclesiasticus 34:25,—Immersionist: "He that *immerses* himself after touching a dead body;" Luther: "That *washeth* himself." Mark 7:5—Immersionist: ("The Pharisees and all the Jews,) when they come from the market, unless they *immerse* themselves, eat not;" Luther: *"wash* themselves." Luke 11:38—Immersionist: "That he had not *immersed* himself;" Luther: *"washed* himself."

5. The Baptist version renders *Baptistes, immerser;* Luther, always *Tauffer, Baptist.*

6. Immersionists say that *Bapto* always properly means,to *dip.* Luther translates Rev. 19:13: "He was clothed with a vesture *sprinkled* with blood."

Those proofs are enough to demonstrate that, judged as a translator, *Luther was no immersionist.*

But it has been urged that Luther has used

taufte, where our translators have "dipped," 2 Kings, v. 14. The fact is, however; that this Verse alone is enough to dispose of the false theory. Our translators have "dipped," it is true ; but as Luther did not translate from our authorized version, that proves nothing. That same authorized version has "dipped" in Rev. 19 :13, where Luther has *"besprenget,"* "sprinkled." The fact is, that if the ravages in the German, on the part of those who are determined to make Luther a Baptist, or an Anabaptist, against his will, are not arrested, they will not leave a word in that language, once deemed somewhat copious, which will express any mode of reaching the human body by water, except by dipping; *"begiessen"* and *"taufen"* are disposed of, and *"besprengen"* can be wiped out exactly as *"taufen"* has been.

The question, however is worth a moment's attention, Why Luther used the Word *"taufte"* in 2 Kings, v. 14? The word *"ta-bhal"* is used sixteen times, but Luther never translated it *"taufen"* except in this place. It is also noticeable that in this place alone does the Septuagint translate *"ta-bhal"* by *"baptizo."* The Vulgate considers it as equivalent in meaning to *"ra-hhatz,"* of the preceding verses; and translates it *"lavit"* washed. The Targum considers the two words as equivalent. So does the Syriac, and so the Arabic. Paginus' version gives to both the same meaning, but marks the distinction between their form by translating *"rahhatz"* *"lavo,"* and *"ta-bhal"* *"abluo."* In his Thesaurus, he gives as a definition of *"ta-bhal"* *"lavare, baptizare,"* and translates it in 2 Kings, V. 14, *"lavit se"* washed himself.

Origen, and many of the Fathers, had found in the washing of Naaman a foreshadowing of Baptism. De Lyra, Luther's great favorite as an expositor, expressly calls this washing—2 Kings, v. 14—a receiving of Baptism. Luther saw in it the great idea of Baptism—the union of water with the word, as he expressly tells us, in commenting on the passage, in his exposition of the cxxii. Psalm.[185] The word *"taufte"* therefore, is to be translated here, as everywhere else in Lather's Bible, not by immerse, but by "baptize." Naaman baptized himself, *not* dipped himself in Jordan, is Luther's meaning. The Hebrew, *tabhal,* Luther translates fourteen times, by *tauchen,* to dip, in accordance with its accepted etymology. But he also translates what he regarded as its participle, by color or dye, Ezek. 23:15. According to the mode of reasoning, whose fallacy we are exposing, wherever Luther uses *"taufen,"* We may translates it "to dye;" for the etymological force of a word, according to this, is invariable, and all true translations of it must have the same meaning.

Bapto Luther translates by *"tauchen* and *eintauchen,"* to dip, dip in; but he also translates it by *"besprengen,"* (Rev. 19:13,) to sprinkle; but, according to this mode of reasoning, *tauchen* and *taufen* both being equivalents, *taufen* is sprinkling, and Baptism is sprinkling, and dipping is sprinkling. By the way in which it is proved that *Taufe* is immersion, may be proved that both *Taufe* and immersion are sprinkling. *Baptizo,* Luther never translated by *tauchen,* nor by any word which would be understood by the readers of his version to mean immersion. Whatever may be the *etymology* of *taufe,* its *actual use* in the German language did not make it equivalent to *immersion.* Sprinkling *(besprengen)* or pouring *(begiessen)* were called *taufe.* If Luther believed that the *actual* (not the primary or etymological) force of the word made immersion necessary, he was bound before God and the Church to use an unambiguous term. It is not true that *"tauchen"* or *"eintauchen"* had, either then or now, that very trifling and vulgar sense, which it is alleged

---

[185] Leip. 3. Edit. V. 461.

unfitted them over against *"taufen,"* to be used to designate immersion. Luther uses them in his Bible, and, when in his liturgies, he means to designate immersion, these Words are the very words he employs.

Luther used the ancient word *Taufen,* because, in the fixed usage of the German, *Taufen* meant, to baptize. Whatever may have been the etymology of it, we find its ecclesiastical use fixed before the ninth century. Otfried so uses it, A. D. 868. Eberhard and Maass, in their great Synonymik of the German, say: "After *Taufen* was limited to this ecclesiastical signification, it was no longer used for *Tauchen,* and can still less be used for it now, that *Taufen* (Baptism) is no longer performed by *Eintauchen* (immersion)."

The propositions which Luther used in connection with *"taufen"* show that he did not consider it in its *actual use* as a synonym of immerse: to baptize *with* water *(mit) with* the Holy Spirit, *(mit.)* John baptized *with* water, *(mit);* baptized under Moses *(unter) with* the cloud, *(mit.)* It is not English, to talk of immersing *with* water; nor would it be German to follow *"tauchen"* or *"eintauchen"* by *"mit;"* nor any more so to use *"mit"* after *"taufen,"* if *taufen* meant to immerse.

Furthermore, Luther has twice, 1 Cor. 15:29, "To baptize *over* the dead," *(über,)* which he explains to refer to the baptism of adults over the graves of the martyrs.

But Luther has not left us to conjecture what he considered the proper German equivalent for *baptizo* and *baptismos,* in their *actual use*—how much their actual use settled as to the *mode* of Baptism. *Five* times only he departs from the rendering by *Taufe,* or *Taufen,* but not once to use *"tauchen,"* but invariably to use *Wuschen,* to wash.

Judith 12:8: *Und wusch sich im Wasser,* washed

herself, (Gr.: *Ebaptizeto;* Vulg.: *Baptizat se.)*

Sir. 34:30, (25:) *Wer sich wascht,* he who washes himself, (Gr.: *Baptizomenos*; Vulg.: *Baptizatur,)* what avails him this washing? *sein Waschen"!* (Gr.: *Loutron.)*

Mark 7:24: *Ungewaschen (aniptois) Handen—sie waschen (nipsontai,) sie waschen sich (baptizontai,) tischen zu waschen (baptismous*;) 7:8: *Zu waschen (baptismous.)*

Luke 11:38: *Das er sich nicht vor dern essen gewaschen hatte (ebaptiste.)*

He translates *baptizo* as he translates *nipto* and *louo.*

Here is the demonstration, that while Luther believed, in common with the great mass of philologists, that the *Etymological force (Laut)* of *baptismos* and *baptisma,* is "immersion," its actual force in biblical use is "washing," without reference to mode. Luther treats it as having the same *generic* force with *louo, pluno* and *nipto,* all of which he translates by the same word, *waschen,* just as our authorized version translates every one of them, *baptizo* included, by wash. With the etymology of the Greek goes also the etymology of the German. The primitive mode of washing, in nations of warm or temperate countries, is usually by immersion. Hence the words in many languages for the two ideas of dipping and washing come to be synonyms—and as the word washing ceases to designate mode, and is equally applied, whether the water be poured, sprinkled or is plunged in, so does the word which, etymologically, meant to dip. It follows the mutation of its practical equivalent, and comes to mean washing, without reference to mode. So our word, bathe, means, *primarily,* to immerse. But we now bathe by "plunge," "douch," or "shower-bath." If the baptismal commission had been given in English, and the word used was Bathe, the person who admitted that the word "bathe" covered all modes of applying water, but who, in a case confessedly a matter of freedom, would prefer immersion as the mode, because it corresponds with the *etymology* of bathe, as well as with its actual use, would do what Luther did in a cognate case, in 1519, of which we are about to speak; but the inference that either regarded the word in question as *meaning* to immerse, or as a synonym of it, would be most unwarranted.

Luther's Etymologies of the Words.

An attempt has been made to show that Luther was an Immersionist, by citing his views of the etymology both of the Greek and German words involved. The citation relied on for this purpose, is from the sermon: *Von Sacrament der Taufe,*[186] which has been thus given: *"Die taufe* (baptism) is, called in Greek, baptismus, in Latin, immersion, that is when any thing is wholly dipped *(ganz ins wasser taucht)* in water which covers it." Further, "according to the import of the word *Tauf,* the child, or any one who is baptized, *(getauft wird)* is wholly sunk and immersed *(sonk und tauft)* in water and taken out again: since, without doubt, in the German language, the word *Tauf* is derived from the word *Tief,* because what is baptized *(taufet)* is sunk deep in water. This, also, the import of *(Tauf)* demands."

This translation is not characterized by accuracy. For example it renders both *"Laut"* and *"Bedeutung,"* by the one word *import,* when Luther expressly distinguishes between *"Laut"* and *"Bedeutung;"* the former referring to the *etymological* or primary literal force of a word, and the latter to the moral significance of a rite.

Further, it mutilates and mistranslates the words, which, literally rendered, are: "Yet it should then be, and WOULD BE RIGHT *(und wär recht,)* that one sink

---

[186] Leipzig Edition, xxii, 139.

and baptize entirely in the water, and draw out again, the child, &c." How different the air of Luther's German, from that of the inaccurate English.

There is another yet more significant fact. It OMITS, out of the very heart of the quotation, certain words, which must have shown that the idea that *"begiessen"* includes immersion is entirely false. The two sentences which are quoted, are connected by these words, which are NOT QUOTED: "And although in many places it is no longer the custom to plunge and dip *(stossen und tauchen)* the children in the font, *(die Tauf,)* but they are poured upon *(begeusst)* with the hand, out of the font *(aus der Tauf.")* Here over against immersion, as the very word to mark the opposite mode, is used that *"begiessen,"* which we have seen referred to immersion. It seems to us inconceivable that any one could read the passage in the original, without having the falsity of the former position staring him in the face.

On the whole passage we remark:

First, That the sermon was published in 1519, among the earliest of Luther's writings, ten years before the Catechism; and when he had not yet made the originals of Scripture the subject of his most careful study, and when his views were still largely influenced by the fathers and Romish theology. It was published five years before he began his translation of the New Testament, and more than twenty before he gave his Bible its final revision. This raises the query whether his views, after the thorough study of the Bible, connected with his translating it, remained unchanged. We have given, and can give again, ample proof that if Luther's meaning in 1519, implies the necessity of immersion, his opinion had undergone a total change before 1529, when the Larger Catechism, whose words are in question, was published.

Secondly, The passage is not pertinent to the

proof of that for which it is urged. Luther designs to give what he supposes to be the *etymological* force of *Baptismos* and *Taufe*— not to show their force in ACTUAL USE.

That Luther affirms not that *Baptismos* and *Taufe* in actual use mean "immersion," but only etymologically, is clear. 1. From the whole vein of argument. As an argument concerning the etymology of the words, it is pertinent; as an argument on the actual use of either, it would be in the highest degree absurd. 2. From his limitation by the word *"Laut"* which means "Etymology," as Luther himself translates it in the Latin, *"Etymologia."* 3. By the fact that twice in these very sentences, Luther uses *Taufe* not in the sense either of immersion or of Baptism, but of "font." 4. That in his translation of the Scriptures he uses *"Taufe"* for "Baptism," without limitation to mode. 5. That in his translation of the Romish Ritual, and wherever else he wishes to indicate the idea of immersion, he never uses *taufe* or *taufen,* always *tauchen* or *untertauchung*. 6. That in the only Baptismal Service properly Luther's own, he directs the water to be poured, with the words, *Ich taufe.* 7. That he repeatedly recognizes the validity of *taufe* by pouring, which would be ridiculous, if *taufe* in actual use meant immersion.

Third. The Latin of Luther's Sermon on Baptism, in the Jena Edition, which excludes every thing of his which was not officially approved, makes very plain the drift of the words quoted. It says: "The noun, Baptism, is Greek, and *can* be rendered *(potest verti,)* in Latin, *Mersio,"*—"That" (*i. e.,* the immersion and drawing out) the *etymology* of the word *(Etymologia nominis – Laut des Wortleins) seems* to demand *(postulate videtur.)* From Luther's opinion on the etymology of the words Baptism and Taufe, the inference is false that he held that Baptism, in the ACTUAL USE of the word, meant immersion, and that the

German word Taufe in ACTUAL USE had the same meaning. To state the proposition is to show its fallacy to any one familiar with the first principles of language,

1. That the etymological force and actual use of words are often entirely different every scholar knows. Carnival is, etymologically, a farewell to meat. Sycophant, etymologically and properly, means a fig-shower; miscreant is a misbeliever; tinsel means "sparkling," (Thetis with the "tinsel-slippered feet," Milton;) Carriage (Acts *21:15,*) means things carried; kindly, (in the Litany,) according to kind; painful, involving the taking of pains; treacle, something made from wild beasts. The German *schlecht,* bad, originally meant good; *selig,* blessed, is the original of our English word silly; the word courteous has its root in a word which meant a cow-pen.

3. The very essence of the philological argument against the necessity of immersion, turns upon this fact. If to admit that *Bapto* and *Baptizo* may, etymologically, mean to dip in, is to admit that, in their ACTUAL USE, they mean exclusively to dip in, then the argument against the Baptists is over.

3. The English words Baptism and baptize, are simply Greek words in an English shape. As this argument puts it, they also mean throughout our authorized version and our whole usage, exclusively immersion or to immerse. So the Baptists contend as to their etymological and native force; but as they, concede that such is not the actual use of them in English, even they, when they translate anew, give us "immersion" and "immerse."

4. If this interpretation of Luther stands, Luther was an immersionist, did teach that immersion is the synonym of Baptism, and is necessary, did hold the "Baptist doctrine of immersion;" but it is admitted that Luther did none of these, therefore this interpretation cannot stand. The argument makes Luther to be

theoretically an immersionist, and only saved by hypocrisy or glaring inconsistency from being an Anabaptist in practice.   A disguised Anabaptist is the Martin Luther which this new philology has given us. The positions are inconsistent with each other, and the arguments for them self-confuting.

What is the real meaning of Luther's words? It is that in its *etymological* and *primary* force *(Laut,)* the German term *taufe,* like the Greek *baptismos,* the Latin *mersio,* means immersion, but he does NOT say, and there is abundant evidence that he did not believe, that in ACTUAL USE, either *taufe* or *baptismos* means exclusively immersion, but, on the contrary, means "washing" without reference to mode. We believe that many scholars of anti-baptist schools will concede that Luther was right in his position as to etymology, as all intelligent Baptists will, and do, concede that the etymological and primary force of any word, may be entirely different from that they have in actual use.

2. Luther, in 1519, drew the inference that it would be right and desirable that the mode of washing should conform to the etymological and primary force, as well as to the actual use of the word. That it would be right, if the Church preferred so to do, is, we think, undisputable; that it is desirable, is, we think, very doubtful, and we can prove such was Luther's attitude to the mode when the Catechisms were written. That immersion is necessary, Luther denied in express terms, in his book on the Babylonish captivity of the same period, (1519.)

3. Luther, in 1519, under the influence of the Romish Liturgy, and of the writings of the Fathers, believed that the moral significance of Baptism, as pointing to the drowning and death of sin, though essentially unaffected by the mode, is yet brought out more clearly in immersion, and at that era *so far* preferred it. In his later Biblical Era, to which his

Catechism belongs, there is ample evidence that this preference was no longer cherished.

This, then, is ill brief the state of the case: The point of Luther's whole argument, in 1519, is, that inasmuch as immersion corresponds With the *etymology* of Baptism, as well as with its actual general use, which embraces every kind of washing, and as a certain signification common to all modes, is most clearly brought out in immersion, it would be right, and *so far* desirable, that *that* mode, though not necessary, but a matter of Christian freedom, should be adopted. Then, as always, he placed the mode of Baptism among the things indifferent, and would have considered it heresy to make the mode an article of faith. In the Church of Rome, some of the older rituals positively prescribe immersion; and in the ritual now set forth in that Church, by authority, there is a direction that, "Where the custom exists of baptizing by immersion, the priest shall immerse the child thrice." Luther, in his Sermon in 1519, expresses his preference for immersion, not on the ground of any superior efficacy, but because of its etymology, antiquity, and significance as a sign; and when he alludes to the fact that the children, in many places, were not so baptized, he does not express the least doubt of the validity of their Baptism.

In his book on the Babylonish Captivity, which appeared in 1520, declaring his preference again for the same mode, he expressly adds: "NOT THAT I THINK IT (immersion) NECESSARY."[187] But this claim of necessity, and this only, is the very heart of the Baptist doctrine. The strongest expressions in favor of immersion occur in Luther's earliest works, and his maturer preference, as expressed in later works, seem to have been no less

---

[187] De Captiv. Babylon: Eccles. Jena Edit., II, 273. *"Non quod necessarium arbitrer"*

decided for pouring as an appropriate mode.

The Liturgies of Luther and of the Lutheran Church.

1. The *Taufbüchlein* of Luther, 1523, is not a Lutheran Ritual, but avowedly only a translation of the Romish service, without change. He declares in the Preface to it, that there was much in it which he would have desired to remove, but which he allowed to remain, on account of the consciences of the weak, who might have imagined that he wished to introduce a new Baptism, and might regard their own Baptism as insufficient. That in this Ritual, therefore, the direction is given to dip the child, *(tauchen,)* only proves that the Romish Ritual had that Rubric.

2. But after this Translation, later in this same year, 1523; Luther issued his own directions for Baptism: *Wie man recht und Verstandlich einen Menschen zum Christenglauben taufen soll.* [188] This document, in the older editions of Luther's works, has been erroneously placed under 1521. The Erlangen edition, the latest and most critical ever issued, gives it its true place, under 1523. In this direction, how RIGHTLY *(recht)* and INTELLIGENTLY *(verstandlich)* to baptize, Luther says: "The person baptizing POURS THE WATER, *(geusst wasser auff,)* and says, *Ego Baptizo te,*" that is, in German, *Ich taüf dich,* (I baptize thee.) POURING, and pouring alone, is described as Baptism, and positively prescribed in the only Ritual of Baptism which is properly Luther's exclusive work.

3. In 1529, the year in which the Catechisms of Luther appeared, in which it is pretended that "the Baptist doctrine of immersion" is taught, he wrote the Seventeen Articles of Schwabach, or Torgau,[189] which

---

[188] Leipz. xxii, 227. Walch x, 2,622. Erlangen xxii, 168.
[189] Leipz. xx 22. Walch xvi 778. Erlangen xxiv 321.

became the basis of the Doctrinal Articles of the Augsburg Confession. In the Ninth Article of these, he says: We baptize WITH water, *(mit Wasser,)*—and Baptism is not mere miserable water, or SPRINKLING and POURING, *(begiessen.)* Here again the *begiessen,* the applying of the water to the person, not the immersing of the person in water, is exclusively spoken of as the mode of Baptism.

4. In the Liturgy of Wittenberg, Luther's own home, (Consistorial Ordnung, 1542; Richter K. O. I, 369,) both dipping and pouring are placed on the same footing in every respect.

5. In the Liturgy of Halle, 1543, (II, 15,) the administrator is expressly left free to use either pouring or dipping.

6. Bugenhagen, in the conjoined work from Luther and himself, (1542,) designing to comfort mothers who had lost their children, says that Baptism of children, by pouring, was prevalent in the Lutheran Churches of Germany, *(das begiessen, sichet man noch bei uns über ganz Deutschland.)*

7. In the Liturgy of the Palatinate of the Rhine, &c, 1556, of which the orignal edition lies before us, it says: "Whether the child shall have water poured on it once or thrice, be dipped or sprinkled, is a MATTER OF INDIFFERENCE, *(mittel massig.)* Yet, that all things may be done in the Church in good order, and to edification, we have regarded it as proper that the child should not be dipped, *(gedaucht,)* but have the water poured upon it, *(begossen werden.")* And in the Rubric: "Then shall the minister pour water *(begiesse)* on the child."

8. The Liturgy of Austria, 1571, directs the Baptism to be performed by pouring or sprinkling. The later usage is so well known, that it is not necessary to multiply citations.

We shall close this part of our discussion with the words of two popular authors of the Lutheran

Church in America. Dr. Schmucker, in his Popular Theology, says, very truly:

"THE QUESTION IS NOT WHETHER BAPTISM BY IMMERSION IS VALID; THIS IS NOT DOUBTED * * BUT THE QUESTION IS WHETHER IMMERSION IS ENJOINED IN SCRIPTURE, AND CONSEQUENTLY IS AN ESSENTIAL PART OF BAPTISM, SO THAT WITHOUT IT NO BAPTISM IS VALID, THOUGH IT CONTAINS EVERY OTHER REQUISITE. ON THIS SUBJECT THE LUTHERAN CHURCH HAS *always* agreed with the great majority of Christian denominations in maintaining the NEGATIVE, and in regarding the QUANTITY of water employed in Baptism as well as the mode of exhibiting it, not essential to the validity of the ordinance."

"The controversy on this subject, (the mode of applying water in Baptism) has always been regarded by the most enlightened divines, INCLUDING LUTHER, Melanchthon, and Chemnitz, as of comparatively inferior importance."

Dr. Benjamin Kurtz, in his work on Baptism, after showing very conclusively that Luther was not an Immersionist, closes his discussion with these words:

"We leave our readers to judge for themselves, from the foregoing extracts, what amount of credit is due to the objection made by SOME OF OUR BAPTIST BRETHREN, that Luther believed in the necessity of submersion to THE EXCLUSION OF EFFUSION, or that he was not decidedly in favor of children's being baptized. To our more ENLIGHTENED READERS WE MAY OWE AN APOLOGY FOR MAKING OUR EXTRACTS SO COPIOUS and dwelling so long on this subject; but THE LESS INFORMED, who have been assailed again and again by this groundless objection, without ability to refute it, will know better how to appreciate our effort."

It is hardly necessary to show that these views of the mode of Baptism were held by all our old divines. A few citations will suffice:

CHEMNITZ :[190] "The verb *Baptizein* does not necessarily import immersion. For it is used John 1: 33, and Acts 1:5 to designate the pouring out of the Holy Spirit. And the Israelites are said, 1 Cor. 10:2, to have been baptized unto Moses, in the cloud and in the sea, who, nevertheless, were not immersed into the sea, nor dipped into the cloud. Wherefore, Paul, a most safe interpreter, says that to baptize, is the same as to purify or cleanse by the laver of water in the Word, Eph. 5:26. Whether, therefore, the water be used by merging, dipping, pouring, or sprinkling, there is a baptizing. And even the washing of hands, couches, and; cups, in which water was employed, whether by merging, dipping or pouring, Mark 7:4, is called Baptism. Nor in the Baptism instituted by Christ is there needed such a rubbing of the body with water, as is needed to remove the filth of the flesh, 1 Pet. 3:21. Since, therefore our Lord has not prescribed a fixed mode of employing the water, there is: no change in the substantials of Baptism, though in different Churches the water is employed in different modes."

FLACIUS ILLYRICUS: "*Baptizo,* by metalepsis, signifies, to *wash, bathe, (abluo, lavo).* Hence, Mark, 7:4, says: 'The Jews have various Baptisms (*i. e.,* washings) of cups, and pots;' and 1 Peter, 3:21, says: 'Our Baptism is not the putting away of the filth of the flesh.' Heb. 6:2, the word Baptism refers to the purifications and washings under the old dispensation." Clavis S. S.

STEPHEN GERLACH says: "Herein Baptism is analogous to circumcision, which, though local, yet availed by its internal action to render the entire person acceptable to God. Thus the laver of regeneration and renewal is most efficacious, whether the person baptized be entirely merged, or dipped, pr some portion

---

[190] On Matt. 28:19. Exam. Concil. Trid. Ed. 1653. See, also, Harmon. Evang. C. xvi.

only of the body be sprinkled, only so that he be baptized with water, in the name of the Father, and of the Son, and of the Holy Spirit." On Matt. 28:19, in Osiander.

GERHARD: "*Baptismos* and *Baptizein* are employed to designate any kind of ablution, whether it be done by sprinkling, pouring, or dipping." Loci Ed. Cotta ix, 68.

QUENSTEDT: "Baptism, in general, signifies washing, or ablution, whether it be done by sprinkling, pouring, clipping, or immersion."

The question of the outward mode in Baptism, is far less serious than the questions as to the internal efficacy of Baptism, its essence, its object, and results. As closely connected with the view of our Church on these points, we shall present some facts in connection with that fundamental Scriptural phrase in regard to Baptism.

"Born of Water and of the Spirit."
The Context.

Our Savior says to Nicodemus, John 3:6: "Except a man be born of water and of the Spirit, he cannot enter into the kingdom of God." Does he refer in these words to Baptism? We think that no one ever could have doubted that there is such a reference, unless he had some preconceived theory of Baptism with which the natural meaning of these words came in conflict. The context and the text alike sustain and necessitate that interpretation which was the earliest, which was once and for ages universal, and to this hour is the general one, the interpretation which accepts these words as setting forth the Christian doctrine of Baptism. We have said the CONTEXT proves this. We will give a few illustrations which seem to us perfectly conclusive on this point:

1. Baptism, in consequence of the ministry of

John the Baptist, was, at the time of the interview between our Lord and Nicodemus, the great absorbing matter of interest in the nation. The baptizing by John was the great religious event of the time. The subject of Baptism, in its relation to the kingdom of God, was the grand question of the hour, and there was hardly a topic on which Nicodemus would be more sure to feel an interest, and on which our Lord would bo more likely to speak.

2. The fact that John baptized was regarded as evidence that he might claim to be the Christ; in other words, it was a settled part of the conviction of the nation that the Messiah would baptize, or accompany the initiation of men into his kingdom with the use of water. "The Jews sent priests and Levites to ask John, Who art thou? And he confessed and denied not; but confessed, I AM NOT THE CHRIST," John 1 ; 20. Not a word had they uttered to imply that they supposed that he claimed to be the Christ, but his answer, to what he knew to he their thought, all the more potently proves, that it was considered that THE CHRIST WOULD BAPTIZE, that the beginning of his kingdom would be in Baptism, that he pre-eminently would be the baptizer. "They asked him, and said unto him, Why baptizest thou then, if thou be not that Christ?" Nicodemus came to settle in his mind, whether Jesus was the Christ. Nothing would be more sure to be a question with him than this: Whether Jesus would claim the right to baptize? The answer of John implied that he baptized by authority of the Messiah, as his divinely appointed forerunner, and provisional administrator of this right of Baptism, whose proper authority lay in Christ alone. Nicodemus would be peculiarly alive to any allusion to Baptism, would be likely to understand as referring to it any words whose obvious meaning pointed to it, and our Lord would the more carefully avoid whatever might mislead him on this point.

3. John continually characterized his work in this way: "I baptize with *water*" Matt. 3:2; Mark 1:8; Luke 3: 16; John 1: 26, 31, 33; Acts 1:5. At this time, and under all these circumstances, the word "water" would be connected specially with Baptism,

4. John had said of Jesus, shortly before this interview of Nicodemus, Mark 1:8: "I indeed have baptized you with water; but he shall baptize you with the Holy Spirit.." Here, before the Ruler of the Jews, was the very person of whom this had been uttered; and when he takes up these words, "water" and "the spirit," it seems impossible that Nicodemus should doubt their allusion to, and their close parallel with, John's words.

5. John had made two kinds of utterances in regard to Christ's work, and we beg the reader to note the great difference between them, for they have been confounded, and gross misrepresentation of them has been the result.

The first of these utterances we have just given, Mark 1: 8. It was made to the body of John's disciples, and the two things he makes prominent are Baptism with water, and Baptism with the Holy Spirit; that is, water and the Spirt;

The other utterance, Matt. 3:7—12, was made to those to whom he said: "O generation of vipers, who hath warned you to flee from the wrath to come?" John knew that, as a class, the Pharisees and Sadducees who came to him were unworthy of Baptism, yet as there were exceptions, and as he could not search hearts, he baptized them all. Nevertheless, he says: "Every tree which bringeth not forth good fruit, is hewn down and cast into the *fire.* I indeed baptize you with water, but he that cometh after me shall baptize you with the Holy Spirit and with *fire.* Whose fan is in his hand, and he will thoroughly purge his floor, and gather the wheat into his garner, but he will burn up the chaff with

unquenchable *fire."* When we look at these words in
their connection, remember the class of persons
addressed, and notice how the Baptist, in the way in
which the word "fire" runs, fixes its meaning here,
nothing seems clearer than this, that John has in view
not the work of the Holy Spirit in the individual, but his
great work in the mass, and not his purifying power in
those who are blessed by it, but his purifying power
shown in the removal and destruction of the evil. The
wind created by the fan descends alike upon the wheat
and the chaff; both are alike baptized by it, but with
wholly different results. The purifying power of the air
is shown in both. It is a single act, indeed, which
renders the wheat pure by removing the impurity of
the chaff. "You," says the Savior to the generation of
vipers, "shall also be baptized With the Holy Spirit." His
work shall be to separate you from the wheat. You, too,
shall be baptized with fire: the fire which *destroys* the
impurity which has been separated by the Spirit. See
also Luke 3:9—17. The addition of the word "fire" marks
with awful significance what is the DISTINCTION OF THE
BAPTISM OF THE WICKED, AND SUCH AN IDEA, AS THAT
THE CHILDREN OF GOD ARE BAPTIZED WITH FIRE, is not to
be found in the New Testament. The only thing that
looks like it is Acts 2: 3, where it is said, "There
appeared unto them cloven tongues like as of fire, and
it sat upon each of them," but the fire here was
symbolical of the character of the TONGUES of the
Apostles, of the fervor with which they glowed, and of
the light which they shed, in the varied languages in
which they spoke. John spoke of the Holy Spirit and
fire, when he addressed those who were not to enter
the kingdom of God. When he addressed true disciples,
he associated water and the Spirit. When he spoke to
the former, it was of the Spirit first, and then of the fire.
When he speaks to the latter, it is of water first, and
then of the Spirit; the one class is to be baptized with

the Spirit and with fire, and are lost; the others are baptized with water and with the Spirit, and will enter the kingdom of God. When John contrasted his Baptism with that of the Savior, he meant not this: I baptize with water only, without the Spirit, and he will baptize with the Spirit only, and not with water; he meant: I baptize with water; that is all I can do in my own person, but he who in his divine power works with me now, and baptizes with the provisional measure of the Holy Spirit, will yet come in his personal ministry, and then he will attend the Baptism of water, with the full gospel measure of the Spirit. When, our Lord, therefore; taking up as it were and opening still further the thought of John, adopts his two terms in the same connection in which he had placed them, he meant that Nicodemus should understand by "water" and the "Spirit" the outward part of Baptism, and that Divine Agent, who in it, with it, and under it, offers his regenerating grace to the soul of man.

6. It is not to be forgotten that Nicodemus was asking for a fuller statement of the doctrine of the new birth. He asked: "How can a man be born when he is old?" The emphasis is not on the word "CAN" alone, as if he meant to express a doubt of the truth of our Savior's proposition; the emphasis rests also on the word "HOW." He meant to say: A man cannot be born again in the natural sense and ordinary way. How then, in what sense, and by what means, CAN he be born again? It is impossible that one interested in grace itself should not be alive to its means. For our Savior not to have made an allusion to any of the divine modes as well as to the Divine Agent of the change, would seem to make the reply a very imperfect one. But if any one of the means of grace is alluded to, the allusion is certainly in the word "water;" and admitting this, the inference will hardly be resisted that "Baptism" is meant.

7. The entire chapter, after the discourse with Nicodemus, is occupied with *baptisms, baptismal questions, and baptismal discourses.*

a. In verse 23, the word "water" occurs: "John was baptizing in Ænon, because there was much *water* there.

b. It is not unworthy of notice, that immediately following the conversation of our blessed Lord with Nicodemus, come these words *"After these things* came Jesus and his disciples unto the land of Judea, and there he tarried with them *and baptized."*

c. John's disciples and the Jews came to him and said: "Rabbi, he to whom thou bearest witness, *behold the same baptizeth,* and all men come to him." Then John replies: "Ye yourselves bear me witness, that I said, *I am not the Christ,* but that I am sent before him." The authority for John's Baptism was secondary, derived from Christ. Christ now takes it into his own hands, and prepares to endow it with the fullness of the gifts of his Spirit.

The Text.

The context of these words demonstrate that by "water" our Savior meant Baptism. The evidence of the text itself, is equally decisive that this is his meaning. It is conceded by all, that if the word "water" be taken literally, it means "Baptism;" hence, all those who deny that it refers to Baptism understand it figuratively, and in that fact acknowledge that to prove that it is to be taken literally, is to prove that it refers to Baptism.

We remark, then,

1. That to take the word "water," figuratively, makes an incongruity with the idea of a birth. It is said that water here is the figure of the cleansing and purifying power of the Holy Spirit. But there is an incongurity in such an interpretation. Had the Savior meant this, he would naturally have said: Except a man

be *cleansed,* or *washed* with water, not "born of" it.

2. One of the figurative interpretations is in conflict with the evident meaning of the word "Spirit" here. For it is clear from the whole connection, that the Spirit here means the Holy Spirit as a person. In the next verse it is said: "That which is born of the SPIRIT is Spirit," and in the 8th verse: "So is every one that is born of the SPIRIT." No sound interpreter of any school, so far as we know, disputes that the word "Spirit," in these passages, means the Holy Spirit as a person; and nothing is more obvious than that the word in the 5th verse means just what it does in the following ones. But if "water" is figurative, then the phrase water and Spirit, means, in one of the figurative interpretations, "spiritual water;" that is, the substantive Spirit is used as an adjective, and not as the name of a person. This false interpretation makes the phrase mean "spiritual water," and Baptism and the Holy Spirit both vanish before it. In its anxiety to read Baptism out of the text, it has read the Holy Spirit out of it, too.

3. Another figurative interpretation turns the words the other way, as if our Savior had said: "Born of the Spirit and water," and now it means not that we are to be born again of "spiritual water," but that we are to be born again of the "aqueous or water-like Spirit." But not only does such a meaning seem poor and ambiguous, but it supposes the one term, "Spirit," to be literal, and the other "water," to be figurative; but as they are governed by the same verb and preposition, this would seem incredible, even apart from the other cogent reasons against it. In common life, a phrase in which such a combination was made, would be regarded as absurd.

4. The term "to be born of" leads us necessarily to the same result.

a. The phrase is employed in speaking of natural birth, as in Matt. 1:16: "Mary *of* whom *was born*

Jesus."

Luke 1: 35: "That holy thing which shall *be born* of thee, shall be called the Son of God." So in this chapter, "that which is *born of* the flesh."

b. It is employed to designate spiritual birth. Thus John 1:13: ("the sons of God) *were born* not of the blood, nor of the will of the flesh, nor of the will of man, but of God." Here no symbolical title is used, but the literal name of the Author of the new birth. So in this chapter, v. 8: "So is every one that is *born* of the Spirit." John, in his gospel and epistles, uses the phrase "to be born of" fifteen times. In fourteen of them, it is not pretended that any of the terms used to designate the cause of the birth is symbolical. The fifteenth instance is the one before us.

The phrase to "be born of" is never connected elsewhere in the New Testament with terms indicative of the means or cause of birth, which are symbolical in their character. The whole New Testament usage is in conflict with the supposition, that it is here linked with a symbolical term.

"Born of God" is used some eight or nine times. "Born of the Spirit" is used twice, and these, with the words before us, exhaust the New Testament use of the phrase.

Without the context, then, the text itself would settle the question, and demonstrate that our Lord referred to Baptism.

The Parallels.

The words of our Lord Jesus to Nicodemus are the keynote to the whole body of New Testament representation in regard to the necessity and efficacy of Baptism. The view which regards the words "Born of water and of the Spirit" as referring to Baptism, is sustained and necessitated by the whole body of PARALLELS in the gospels and epistles. Let us look at a few of these:

1. In Titus 3:5, Paul, speaking of God our Savior, says: "He saved us, by the washing of regeneration, and renewing of the Holy Spirit."

Here the subject is the same as in John 3:5, the new birth, or regeneration. There is a parallel between "born of God," and "regeneration," and "renewing;" between "water" and "washing," or laver. "The Spirit" in the one is parallel with "the Holy Spirit" in the other, and "Entering, into the kingdom of heaven" in the one has its parallel in the other, in the words, "He saved us." What a beautiful comment does Paul make on our Lord's work. Take up the words in John and ask Paul their meaning. What is it to be "born again?" Paul replies, "It is to experience regeneration and renewing." What is the "water," of which our Lord says we must be born? It is the washing of regeneration. What is the Spirit? Paul replies, "The Holy Spirit." What is it to enter the kingdom of God? It is to be saved.

2. So in Ephes. 5:26: "Christ loved the Church and gave himself for it, that he might sanctify and cleanse it with the washing of water by the Word."

In these words the new birth is represented as sanctifying and cleansing; the "water" is expressly mentioned; to be "born of water" is explained as a "sanctifying and cleansing with the washing of water," and the "Word" as a great essential of Baptism and organ of the Holy Spirit in it, is introduced.

3. Hebrews 10: 21: "Let us draw near with a true heart, in full assurance of faith, having our hearts sprinkled from an evil conscience, and our bodies washed with pure water."

Here Baptism is regarded as essential to having a true heart and full assurance of faith, and the mode in which "water" is used is defined in the words, "having our bodies, washed with pure water."

4. In 1 John 5: 6—8, speaking of Jesus: "This is

he that came by *water* and blood, not by *water* only, but by water and blood. And it is the Spirit that beareth witness, because the Spirit is truth. And there are three that bear witness on earth, the Spirit, and the water, and the blood."

Here is a most decisive confutation by John himself of the glosses put upon his Master's words. They demonstrate that "water" and "Spirit" are not one. "There are *three* that bear witness, the Spirit, *and* the water, and the blood."

5. The parallel in St. Peter, is also very important. 1 Pet. 3: 21—22: "The Ark, wherein few, that is, eight, souls were saved by water. The like figure whereunto *even* Baptism doth now save us."

The water lifted the Ark above it, away from the death which overwhelmed the world. It separated the eight souls from the lost, and saved them while it destroyed the others. Here the Apostle, speaking of "souls saved by water," declares that Baptism, in such sense, corresponded with the deluge, fiat we say of it also, "It saves *us,*"—the implication being irresistible—that the whole thought involved is this: in the Church, as in the Ark, souls are saved by water, that is, by Baptism. Having said so great a thing of Baptism, the Apostle adds: "Not the putting away of the filth of the flesh, but the answer of a good conscience toward God." That is, it is not as a mere outward purifier, or ceremonial washing, Baptism operates. Its gracious effects are conditioned on the state of heart of him to whom they are offered, He who in faith accepts Baptism in its purifying energy through the Spirit of God, also receives it in its saving result.

6. The words of our Lord Jesus, elsewhere, fully sustain the view which the Church takes of his meaning in John 3:5. In his final commission he charges the Apostles "to *baptize*" the nations, Matt. 28:19, and connects with it the promise: "He that believeth, and is

baptized, shall be saved;" and adds: "but he that believeth not shall be damned," Mark 16:16.

Reader, ponder, we beseech you, these words. Do not separate what God hath joined together. Who shall be saved? First, He only that *believeth.* That is decisive against the idea that Sacraments operate apart from the spiritual state of the recipient. It is a death-blow to formalism— a death-blow to Rome, and to Oxford. We are justified by faith; that is written with a sunbeam in the words: "He that believeth * * shall be saved." But is that all the Savior said? No! he adds, "AND IS BAPTIZED, shall be saved." Who dares read a "NOT" in-the words, and make our Savior say, "He that believeth, and is NOT baptized, shall be saved?" But the man who says "Baptism *is in no sense* necessary to salvation," does contradict the words of our Lord. But if it be granted that *in any sense* our Lord teaches that Baptism is necessary to salvation, then it makes it highly probable that the same doctrine is asserted in John 8:5. The reader will please notice that we are not now attempting to settle the precise meaning of either the words in John or the parallels. Our question now simply is, What is the *subject* when our Savior speaks of water and the Spirit?

7. In the minds of the Apostles the doctrines of our Lord, of the necessity *in some sense,* (we are not inquiring now, in *what* sense or with what limitations) of Baptism, to salvation was ever present. When the multitudes said to Peter, and to the rest of the Apostles, "Men and brethren, what shall we do?" then Peter said unto them, "Repent and be baptized, every one of you, in the name of the Lord Jesus Christ, for the remission of sins, and ye shall receive the gift of the Holy Spirit." Now, mark—first, that Baptism and the Holy Spirit are separately spoken of, as in John 3:5; second, that Baptism is represented as a means or condition of receiving the gift of the Holy Spirit; third, that besides

repentance, Baptism is enjoined as necessary; fourth, that it is clearly set forth as in *some sense* essential to the remission of sins.

8. The Apostles and other ministers of the Lord Jesus baptized all persons: "When they believed Philip preaching "the things concerning the kingdom of God, they were baptized," Acts 8:12. When Philip preached Jesus to the eunuch, he said, "What doth hinder me to be baptized?" And Philip said, "If thou believest with all thine heart, thou mayest;" not, as some would say now, "If thou believest with all thine heart, there is no need of being baptized." Thus, Lydia and her household; the Jailor and his household.

No matter where or when the Spirit of God wrought his work in men, they were baptized, as if for some reason, and in some sense it was felt that this was necessary to an entrance on the kingdom of God.

9. Ananias said to Saul, after announcing to him the commission which God gave him: "And now why tarriest thou? Arise, and be baptized, and wash away thy sins, calling on the name of the Lord," Acts 22:16.

Here Baptism is represented as necessary, in *some sense,* even to a converted man, as a means, *in some sense,* of washing away sins.

10. As resonances of the wonderful words of our Lord, we have the Apostle's declaration: "So many of us as were baptized into Jesus Christ, were baptized into his death, therefore we are buried with him by baptism into death. By one Spirit are we all baptized into one body. For as many of you as have been baptized into Christ have put on Christ."

Thus comparing God's Word with itself do we reach a sure ground. Context, text, and parallel, the great sources of a sound interpretation of the living oracles, all point to one result, in determining what our Lord spoke of when he said: "Except a man be born of water and of the Spirit, he cannot enter into the kingdom of God."

The Resorts of Interpreters.

The form of speech to which resource has most frequently been had here to get a figure out of the words, is that which is called "HENDIADYS;" that is, the phrase in which *one* (Hen) is presented *by* (dia) *two,* (dys.) That is to say, *two* nouns are used where one would answer, by presenting the idea of the other in an adjective form; Thus Virgil says: "We offered drinks in bowls and gold:" that is, in golden bowls, or bowl-shaped gold. By this hendiadys, the Savior is said here to have meant "spiritual water," or "the water-like Spirit."

Now let us look at this "hendiadys" by which it is proposed to set aside the natural meaning of our Savior's words. We remark:

1. That, after a careful search, we cannot find a solitary instance (leaving this out of question for a moment) in which it is supposed that the Savior used the form of speech known as hendiadys. It was not characteristic of him.

2. Neither was it of John the Evangelist, whose style is closely formed upon that class of our Lord's discourses which he records in his gospel.

3. Nor is it characteristic of the style of any of the New Testament writers. But three instances of it are cited in the entire New Testament by Glass in his Sacred Philology, and in every one of those three, the language is more easily interpreted without the hendiadys than with it. Winer, the highest authority on such a point, says, in regard to hendiadys in the New Testament: "The list of examples alleged, *does* not, when strictly examined, *furnish one* that is unquestionable."[191]

---

[191] Gramm. of N. T. Diction; Transl. by Masson. Smith,

4. The passage in Matt. 3:11: "He shall baptize you with the Holy Spirit and with fire," is the only one in which it is pretended that a parallel is found with the one before us; but we have shown in a former part of, this article, that there is no hendiadys there; the fire and the Holy Spirit are distinct subjects. The persons addressed were neither to be baptized exclusively with the Holy-Spirit-like fire, or the fire-like Holy Spirit, but just as our Lord says, with both; with the Holy Spirit *and* with fire, the former in his personality separating them as the breath of the purifier's fan, and the latter consuming them as the purifier's flame.

5. But we have a little more to say in regard to this hendiadys; and that is, that if we even concede that it is used here, it does not help the figurative interpretation at all. For look at its real character a moment. Hendiadys does not affect at all the question of the *literalness* or figurativeness of the terms embraced in it; it does not change their *meaning,* but simply their form. Take, for example, the illustration we gave from Virgil: "bowls" and "gold" are both literal; and to have "golden bowls," you must have literal gold as well as literal bowls; not gold analogous to a bowl, or a bowl like to gold. So Lucan says of a horse: "He champed the brass and bit;" that is, the brass-formed bit; but the brass was real, and the bit was real; it does not mean the brass-like bit, or the bit-like brass. So, in Acts 14:13, it is said that the expression "oxen and garlands," is a hendiadys, and means "garlanded oxen." We are not quite sure that it does; but if it does, it means there were literally garlands and literally oxen. Oxen is not figurative, meaning strength, of which the ox is a symbol; nor does "garlands" mean "honored," though garlands are an image of honor. It does not mean that they brought honored strength, or strong

honor, to the gates; but hendiadys or ho hendiadys, it involves equally that there were oxen and garlands. So here, even supposing a hendiadys, we must none the less have literally water, and literally the Spirit.

The only thing hendiadys proves, is, that the things it involves are not separated; and if we suppose a hendiadys here, it leaves both the water and the Spirit as literal terms, and only involves this, that they are conjoined in the one birth. In other words, hendiadys only makes a slight bend in the route, and brings us after all to the same result as the most direct and artless interpretation, to wit, that our Savior referred to Baptism in his words to Nicodemus.

Another resort, more extreme than the one we have just disposed of, is that of the EPEXEGESIS, that is to suppose that the "AND" gives the words this force: "Born of water, THAT is TO SAY, of the Spirit." It is contended that it is parallel to such an expression as this: "God and our Father," which means: "God, *that is to say,* our Father." In the epexegesis, one thing is spoken of in more than one aspect, and, hence, under more than one term. For instance, in the phrase we have quoted: "God and our Father" means: That Being who is God, *as to his nature,* and Father, *as to his relation to us,* God essentially, and Father relatively; in a word, *both* God and Father. It does not make the term God metaphorical, and the term Father the literal substitute for it. If an epexegesis, therefore, were supposable in John 3:5, the phrase could only mean: Born of that which is water, as to its outer part, and Spirit, as to its internal agent; that is, *both* water and Spirit. It is, therefore, of no avail to resort to the epexegesis here, even if it were allowable. But it is not allowable. There is not an instance, so far as we know, in human language, in which a noun used metaphorically is conjoined by a simple "and" with a term which is literal and is meant to explain it. In a word, the tricks of a false interpretation, which are sometimes very specious, utterly fail in this case. Our Lord has fixed the sense of his words so surely, that the unprejudiced who weigh them calmly, cannot be at a loss as to their meaning.

THE DOCTRINES OF ORIGINAL SIN AND OF BAPTISM, IN THEIR RELATIONS TO EACH OTHER.

The doctrine of our Church on these points, will be found summarily stated in the Second Article of the Augsburg Confession. It is placed in its historical relation between the first Article which treats of God, in his essence and in his creative and providential work, and the third, which is of the Son of God, the Redeemer. Between these naturally comes the doctrine of sin, and especially of sin in its original spring, both in the first man and in each individual of his posterity.

Analysis of the Article.

The Article of the Confession, if analyzed, will be found to present, either in so many words, or by just inference, the following points:

1. The doctrine of original sin is taught with *great unanimity* by our Churches.

2. The *time* of the operation of original sin is the whole time subsequent to the fall of Adam.

3. The *persons affected* by it are all human beings born in the course of nature.

4. The *mode of the perpetuation* of original sin, is that of the natural extension of our race.

5. The *great fact asserted* in this doctrine, is this, that all human beings are conceived and born in, and with sin.

6. This sin *results or reveals its working* in these respects.

a. That all human beings are born without the

fear of God.

b. They are born without trust toward God.

c. That they are born with concupiscence, that is, that from their birth they are full of evil desire and evil propensity.

d. That they can have, by nature, no true fear nor love of God, nor faith in God.

7. The *essence* of original sin involves, that this disease or vice of origin is *truly sin.*

8. The *natural consequence* of this original sin, is this: that it condemns and brings now, also, eternal death.

9. This natural consequence is *actually incurred* by all who are not *born again.*

10. When the new birth takes place it is invariably wrought by the *Holy Spirit.*

11. This new birth by the Holy Spirit, has Baptism as an *ordinary* means.

12. Baptism is the *only* ordinary means of *universal* application.

13. Our Church condemns, first, The Pelagians, and, secondly, all others who deny that the vice of origin is sin, and thirdly, all who contend that man by his own strength, as a rational being, can be justified before God; fourthly, and who thus diminish the glory of the merit of Christ and of his benefits.

It is with the Eleventh of these theses, alone, that we desire for the present to occupy the attention of the reader.

Relations of Baptism *to Original Sin. The Eleventh Thesis.*

11. This new birth, by the Holy Spirit, has Baptism as one of its ordinary means.

The part of the Second Article of the Augsburg Confession which comes under discussion in this thesis is that which asserts that original sin brings eternal death to all those who are not born again *of* Baptism and of the Holy Spirit. We have shown the absolute necessity of being born again: we have seen that the Holy Spirit is absolutely essential to that new birth: it now remains to explain and vindicate our Confession in its declaration that the new birth must also be of Baptism.

As this is one of the points specially objected to, and as these words have been omitted in the Definite Platform, which, so far as its omission is evidence, denies not only the necessity of Baptism, but the necessity altogether either of the *new birth* or of the *Holy Spirit* to remove the results of original sin, we may be pardoned for dwelling at some length upon it. The doctrine of our Church, in regard to Baptism, is one of the few fundamental points, on which any part of evangelical Christendom avowedly differs from her. We propose to give first some historical matter bearing upon the origin and meaning of these words in our Confession. We shall present these chronologically.

I. The Marburg Articles.

1529. The fifteen doctrinal articles of Luther, prepared at the Colloquy at Marburg, October 3rd, may be regarded as the remoter basis of the doctrinal articles of the Augsburg Confession. The fourth, fifth, and sixth of these articles, exhibit in full the relations of original sin and salvation. They run thus: "In the *fourth* place we believe that original sin is inborn in us, and inherited by us from Adam, and is a sin of such kind that it condemns all men, and if Jesus Christ had not come to our help with his life and death, we must have died eternally therein, and could not have come to the kingdom and blessedness of God. In the *fifth* place we believe that we are redeemed from this sin and from all other sins, and from eternal death, if we believe on the Son of God, Jesus Christ, who died for us, and without this faith we cannot be absolved from a single sin by any work, condition, or Order. In the *sixth* place, that this faith is a gift of God, which we can gain by no antecedent work or merit, nor can reach by any power of our own, but the Holy Spirit gives and furnishes it where he will, in our hearts, when we hear the gospel or word of Christ. In the *seventh* place, this, faith is our righteousness before God."[192]

II. The Seventeen Doctrinal Articles.

1530. These Marburg Articles, which were signed by LUTHER, MELANCHTHON, ZWINGLE and ŒCOLAMPADIUS, and, the other leading theologians on both sides, were laid by Luther as the ground work of the Seventeen Doctrinal Articles, which were prepared the same year, and which appeared in 1530. These Seventeen Articles are the direct basis of the doctrinal portion of the Augsburg Confession, of which Luther, with far more propriety than Melanchthon, can be styled the author. Melanchthon was the *composer* of the Augsburg Confession rather than its *author.* In the fourth of these Articles, Luther says: "Original sin would condemn all men who come from Adam, and would separate them forever from God, had not Jesus Christ become our representative, and taken upon himself this sin and all sins which follow upon it, and by his sufferings made satisfaction therefor, and thus utterly removed and annulled them in himself, as is clearly taught in regard to this sin in Psalm fifty-first and Romans fifth."[193]

III. The German Edition of 1533.

1533. In Melanchthon's German Edition of the

---

[192] The Articles are given in full in Rudelbach's Reformation, Lutherthum u. Union, p. 665.
[193] Jena Ed. v. 14. Mentzer, Exeges. Aug. Conf., p. 42.

Confession, in 1533, the only edition in the German in which any variations were made by him, and which has never been charged with deviating in meaning in any respect from the original Confession, this part of the Article runs thus: "(Original sin) condemns all those under God's wrath, who are not born again through Baptism and faith in *Christ,* through the *gospel* and Holy Spirit.."[194]

IV. Meaning of the Confession.

From these historical parallels and illustrations, certain facts are very clear as to the meaning of the Confession.

Drift of the Article.

1. The article teaches us what original sin would do if there were no redemption provided in Christ. The mere fact that Christ has wrought out his work, provides a sufficient remedy, *if it be applied, to save every human creature* from the *effects of original sin.* Let not this great fact be forgotten. Let it never be left out of the account in looking at the mystery of original sin, that there is an ample arrangement by which the redemption of every human creature from the results of original sin could be effected, that there, is no lack in God's *provision* for saving every one of our race from its results. "Our Lord Jesus Christ, by the grace of God, tasted death for *every man."*

Is any Man Lost for Original Sin only?

2. It is not the doctrine of our Confession that any human Creature has ever been, or ever will be, lost purely on account of original sin. For while it supposes that original sin, if *unarrested,* would bring death, it

---

[194] Weber's Edit. Weimar, 1781.

supposes it to be arrested, certainly and ordinarily, by the Holy Spirit, through the divine means rightly received, and throws no obstacle in the way of our hearty faith, that in the case of infants dying without the means, the Holy Spirit, in his own blessed way, directly and extraordinarily, may make the change that delivers the child from the power of indwelling sin.

Luther in his marginal note on John 15:22, says: "Through Christ original sin is annulled, and NO MAN, since Christ's coming, is condemned, unless he will not forsake it, (original sin,) that is, will not believe."

Who are Mainly Referred to in this Article?

3. It seems very probable, from the parallels, that the Confessors had mainly, though not exclusively, in their eye in this particular part of the article, original sin as developing itself in *actual sin in the adult,* and requiring the work of the Holy Spirit to save men from its curse. Hence the illustrious Pfaff, in his brief, but very valuable, notes on the Confession, says: "The language here has chiefly *(maxime)* reference to adults who despise Baptism," and such is unquestionably the drift of the form in which Melanchthon puts it in the edition of 1533.

Baptism: In what sense Necessary.

4. The Confession does not teach that the outward part of Baptism regenerates those who receive it. It says, that it is necessary to be born again of Baptism *and of the Holy Spirit.* It is evident from this, that it draws a distinction between the two. It implies that we may have the *outward* act of Baptism performed, and not be born again; but confessedly we cannot have the saving energy of the Holy Ghost exercised upon us, without being born again, whether ordinarily, in Baptism, or, extraordinarily, without

Baptism. Hence, while the doctrine of the Confession is that the new *birth itself* is *absolutely* essential to salvation, and that the energy of the Holy Spirit is *absolutely* essential to the new birth, it is not its doctrine that the *outward part* of Baptism is *absolutely* essential, nor that *regeneration* necessarily attends it. The *necessity* of the *outward* part of Baptism is not the absolute one of the Holy Spirit, who himself *Works* regeneration, but the *ordinary* necessity of the precept, and of the means. God has enjoined it, has connected his promise with it, and makes it one of the ordinary channels of his grace.

Is Baptism Absolutely Necessary?

5. Hence, of necessity, goes to the ground the assumption that the Augsburg Confession teaches that unbaptized infants are lost, or that any man deprived, without any fault of his own, of Baptism is lost. The *absolute* necessity of Baptism has been continually denied in our Church. Luther, as is well known to all readers of his works, denied the absolute necessity of Baptism, as did the other great Reformers of bur Church.

CARPZOV, whose Introduction to our Symbolical Books is a classic, says: "The Augsburg Confession does not say, that unbaptized infants may not be regenerated in an *extraordinary* mode. The harsh opinion of Augustine and of other fathers in regard to this, was based upon a misunderstanding of John. 3:5, for they regarded those words as teaching an *absolute* necessity of Baptism, when in fact that necessity is only *ordinary,* a necessity, which binds us and will not allow us to despise or neglect Baptism, but does not at all bind God to this means, as if he *could* not, or *would* not, in a case of necessity arising in his own providence; perform that in an *extraordinary* way, which in other cases he performs in an *ordinary* one, through means instituted by himself; As, therefore, the texts of Scripture speak of an *ordinary* necessity, so, also, of that same sort of necessity, and of no other, do the Protestants speak in the Augsburg Confession."

It would be very easy to cite evidence on the same point from all our most eminent Lutheran writers on the doctrine of our Church, but it is not necessary here. No one who has read them will need any citations to establish a fact, with which he is so familiar; and yet there are men who tell the world that it is a doctrine of our Church that Baptism is so absolutely essential, that all unbaptized persons are necessarily lost. Such statements involve a lack of ordinary morality on the part of those who make them; for if they are so ignorant as not to know that they are uttering untruths, their pretending to speak of them, as if they knew something about them, shows a complete want of truthfulness.

Infant Salvation in the Lutheran System.

6. The truth is, no system so thoroughly as that of our Church, places the salvation of infants on the very highest ground.

"The *Pelagian* system would save them on the ground of personal innocence, but that ground we had seen to be fallacious." The *Calvinistic* system places their salvation on the ground of divine election, and speaks of *elect* infant, and, hence, in its older and more severely logical shape, at least, supposed not only that some unbaptized, but also that some baptized infants, were lost. The *Baptist* system, which totally withholds Baptism from the infant, and every system which, while it confers the outward rite, denies that there is a grace of the Holy Spirit, of which Baptism is the ordinary channel, are alike destitute of their theory of any *means* actually appointed of God to heal the soul of the infant. The *Romish* system, too Pelagian to think that original sin could bring the pains of death, and too tenacious of the external rite, to concede that an infant can be saved without it, reaches the idle theory, that the unbaptized infant is neither positively lost, in the fullest sense, nor is it saved. It is neither in heaven nor hell, but in a dreary *limbo.* How beautiful and self-harmonious over against all these, is the view of our Church. It knows of no non-elect infants, but believes that our children are alike in the eyes of Infinite Mercy, It confesses that all children are sinners by nature, and believes that the Holy Spirit must change those natures. It believes that God has appointed Baptism as the ordinary channel through which the Holy Spirit makes that change in the nature of a child. In the fact that there is an ordinary means appointed, our Church sees the guarantee that God wishes to renew and save children, and *what so powerfully as this,* prompts the blessed *assurance, that if God fails* to reach the child in his ordinary way, he will reach it in some other. The Calvinist *might* have doubts as to the salvation of a dying child, for to him Baptism is not a sure guarantee, and its grace is meant only for the elect; the Baptist *ought* to have doubt on his system, as to whether an infant can be saved, for his system supposes that God has no appointed means for conferring grace on it, and the presumption is almost irresistible, that where God has no *means* to do a thing, he does not intend to do it; but the Lutheran cannot doubt on this point of such tender and vital interest. The baptized child, he feels assured, is actually accepted of the Savior, and under the benignant power of the Holy Spirit. In infant Baptism is the gracious pledge that God means to save little children; that they have a distinct place in his plan of mercy, and that he has a distinct mode of putting them in that place. When, then, in the mysterious providence of this Lover of these precious little ones, they are cut off from the reception of his grace, by its ordinary channel, our

Church still cherishes the most blessed assurance, in the very existence of infant Baptism, that in some *other way* God's wisdom and tenderness will reach and redeem them. Our confidence in the uncovenanted mercy of God is strong just in proportion to the tenacity with which we cling to Baptism as an ordinary means, most necessary on our part, if we may possibly have it, or have it given. Because in the green valley and along the Still waters of the *visible* Church, God has made rich provision for these poor sin-stricken lambs; because he has a *fold* into which he gathers them out of the bleak world, therefore, do we believe that if one of them faint ere the earthly hands, which act for Christ, can bring it to the fold and pasture, the great Shepherd, in his own blessed person, will bear to it the food and the water necessary to nurture its undying life, and will take it into the fold on high, for which the earthly fold is meant, at best, but a safeguard for a little while. But the earthly fold itself, reared in the valley of peace which lies along the water which ripples with something of a heavenly music, is a sure token of a love which will never fail of its object, a visible pledge that it is not the will of our Father in heaven that *one* of these little ones should perish. Although these facts may be considered decisive, yet it may not be useless further to look into the question,

Is BAPTISM Necessary to Salvation?

The Augsburg Confession (Art. IX, 1) declares that Baptism is necessary to salvation." Is it justified in so doing? Can we accept a statement apparently so sweeping? Is it a Scripture statement?

In order properly to answer these questions, it is necessary to determine what the Confessors meant. In all human writings, and in the Book of God, occur propositions apparently universal, which are, nevertheless, in the mind of the writer, limited in various ways. What is the meaning of the proposition of our Confession? Is it absolute, and without exceptions, and if it meant to allow exceptions, what are they? The first question we naturally ask, in settling the meaning of our Confession, is,

I. What is Baptism.

The Platform, in defining *what* Baptism it supposes the Church to connect with salvation, designates it as "such WATER BAPTISM."

But what our Church affirms of the blessings of Baptism, she does not affirm of "water Baptism," that is, of the application of water *per se*.

The total efficacy of the sacraments is defined in the Augsburg Confession, (Art. V, 2,) thus, that through them and the word, "as instruments, or means, God gives his Holy Spirit who worketh faith." It would at once remove much of the grossest prejudice against the doctrine of our Church, if it were known and remembered that the Baptism, of whose blessings she makes her affirmative, embraces not merely the external element, but yet more, and pre-eminently, the word; and the Holy Spirit. She regards it as just as absurd to, refer any blessings to Baptism, as *her enemies define* it, as it would be to attribute to swords and guns, the power of fighting battles without soldiers to wield them.

Her first lesson on the subject is: "Baptism is not mere water," (Cat. Min., 361, 2.) "Wherefore," says Luther, (Cat. Maj., 487, 15,) "it is pure knavery and Satanic scoffing, that now-a-days these new spirits, in order to revile Baptism, separate from it the word and institution of God, and look upon it as if it were mere water from the well, and; then, with their childish driveling, ask, 'What good can a handful of water do the soul?' Yes, good friend, who does not know that when you separate the parts of Baptism, water is water?" "Baptism cannot be sole and simple water, (do. 26) mere water cannot have that power." Not by virtue of the water," (do. 29.) "Not that the water (of Baptism) is in itself better than any other water," (do. 14.) So in the Smalcald Articles: "We do not hold with Thomas and the Dominican friars, who, forgetful of the word and the institution of God, say, That God has conferred a spiritual power on Water, which washes away sin through the water," (320, 2.)

"Baptism," says Gerhard,[195] "is the washing of water in the word, in which washing the whole adorable Trinity purifieth from sin him who is baptized, *not by the work wrought (ex opere operato) but by the effectual working of the Holy Spirit coming upon him, and by his own faith.*" Such is the tenor of all the definitions our Church gives of Baptism, from the simple elementary statements of the Catechism up to the elaborate definitions of the great doctrinal systems.

The assumption, then, that what the Church says of Baptism, she affirms of mere water Baptism, rests on a fundamental misapprehension. Whatever is wrought is Baptism, is wrought by the Holy Spirit, through the word, with the water, in the believing soul.

III. Baptism is not always followed by Regeneration. Regeneration not always preceded by Baptism.

"That some adults, by actual impenitence, hypocrisy, and, obstinacy, deprive themselves of the salutary efficacy of Baptism, we freely admit." Gerhard (IX, 170.)

Just as clear as they are in their judgment that Baptism is not necessarily followed by regeneration, are our Churchy and her great divines, in the judgment that Baptism is not necessarily preceded by Baptism, or attended by it.

---

[195] Loci (Cotta) ix, 318.

The Augsburg Confession (Art. V) declares the gospel (as, well as the Sacraments) to be the means whereby the Holy Spirit works and confers faith, and (Art. VII) presents the gospel purely preached (as well as the sacraments) as that whereby the true Church is marked out and made.

"As we came alone through the word of God, to God, and are justified, and no man can embrace the word but by faith, it follows that by faith we are justified." (Apol. 99, 68.)

"The natural man is, and remains, an enemy of God, until, by the power of the Holy Spirit, through the word preached and heard, he is converted, endowed with faith, *regenerated* and renewed." (Form. Concord, 589, 5.)

"We cannot obey the law unless we are *born again* through, the gospel." Apol. Conf. 140, 190. "Faith alone brings us to a new birth." Do. 119, 61. "This faith alone justifies and regenerates." Do. 138, 171. "Regeneration is wrought by faith in repentance." Do. 253.

"When, therefore," says Gerhard (Loc. VIII, 325) "they are baptized, who have already been regenerated through the word, as a spiritual seed, they have no need of regeneration through Baptism, but in them Baptism is a confirmation and sealing of regeneration."

Men may be Unbaptized and be Saved.

When Nicodemus asked, "How can a man be born when, he is old?" Jesus replied, "Of water and of the Spirit," and extends the proposition to all "that which is born of the flesh;" that is, to "all men after the fall of Adam, who are born in the course of nature." (A.C, Art. II.) The necessity of the new birth he clearly predicates upon the fact, that the flesh, which is such by virtue of fleshly birth, requires this change.

We need not stop here to show that in John 3:5,

water means Baptism. The Platform concedes this (p. 31): "The language of the Savior, *doubtless,* refers also to Baptism."

But even critics who deny this, concede that in John 3:6, man is contemplated as the subject of original sin. Those who concede this, (and this all concede,) and who concede that "water" means Baptism, (and this the Platform concedes,) concede that, not only in the phraseology, but in the connection, application and argument of that phraseology, the Augsburg Confession is perfectly justified by the Savior's language, when it says (Art. II,) "this original sin" ("that which is born of the flesh is flesh") "brings now also eternal death" ("cannot see the kingdom of God") "to those who are not born again of Baptism ('water') and of the Holy Spirit." If the case is made out from these word, against the Confession of the Church, it is also made out against the Savior, to whose words it so closely adheres. The dilemma, then, is irresistible, either that both teach it, or that neither does. As regards the effectual overthrow of their own position, it matters little which horn the objectors take. If they take the one, then, on their own concesssion, the Savior teaches Baptismal regeneration; if they take the other, on their own concession the Confession does not teach Baptismal regeneration. Is, then, the inference warranted, that our Savior in his words, and our Confession in its use of them, mean to affirm an absolute and unconditional necessity, that a man shall be born of water, before he can enter into the kingdom of God? We reply, that neither the Savior nor the Confession meant to affirm this, but simply an *ordinary* necessity. "The necessity of Baptism is not *absolute,* but ordinary." Gerhard (IX, 383.) Bellarraine had argued from John 3:5, for the Romish doctrine that unbaptized infants are lost. Gerhard (IX, 287,) replied: "1. The warning of Christ bears not upon the privation of the

Sacrament, but the contempt of it. 2. He describes the ordinary rule, from which cases of necessity are expected. We are bound to the use of the means, but God may show his grace in extraordinary ways."

IV. Are Unbaptized Infants Saved?

How touchingly and consolingly LUTHER wrote upon this topic, is known to all admirers of his writings. Bugenhagen, in an admirable Treatise, which is incorporated in Luther's Works, and was issued with a Preface by him, shows at large, that neither to infants nor adults is the necessity of baptism absolute. "Rather should we believe that the prayers of pious parents, or of the Church are graciously heard, and that these children are received by God into his favor and eternal life. Gerhard, IX. 284.

On the whole dark question of the relation of the heathen world to salvation, the early writers of our Church generally observe a wise caution. Yet even in the school of the most rigid orthodoxy we find the breathings of tender hope. "It is false," says Mentzer, (Oper. I. 959, quoted in Gerhard—, Cotta,) "that original sin in infants out of the Church is an adequate cause of reprobation; for men are never said in Scripture to be reprobated on that account solely. But as faith alone justifies and saves, so also, as Luther says, unbelief alone condemns."

Ægidius Hunnius, whom Gerhard pronounced the most admirable of the theologians of his period, and of whom another great writer says, that by universal consent he holds the third place of merit after Luther, says (*In Quaest.* in Cap. VII. Gen :) "I would not dare to affirm that the little children of heathen, without distinction, are lost for God desireth not the death of any—Christ died for them also," &c. (Quoted in Gerhard IX. 284.)

Our Church, then, does not teach that Baptism

"is necessarily and unavoidably attended by spiritual regeneration," but holds that a man may be baptized, and remain then and forever in the gall of bitterness, and in the bonds of iniquity, and therefore holds as heartily and fully as the Platform, (p. 29) "that baptism in adults does not necessarily effect or secure their regeneration."

V. Baptism not Essential.

In the second place, our Church regards Baptism not as *"essential"* in its proper sense, but as "necessary." That which is properly "essential," allows of no degree of limitation; but that which is "necessary," may be so in various degrees with manifold limitations.

It is *"essential"* to our Redemption that Christ should die for us; therefore, without limits of any kind, we affirm that ho human being could be saved without his atoning word.

It is "necessary" that we should hear the gospel, for it is the power of God unto salvation; but the necessity of hearing is limited in various ways. It does not comprehend both infants and adults, as that which is essential does.

VI. But Necessary.

The Augsburg Confession (Art. IX.) says, not that Baptism is essential, but simply that it is necessary—to which the Latin, not to show the *degree* of necessity, but merely its *object,* adds *"to salvation."*

In later editions of the Confession, Melanchthon, to remove the possibility of misconstruction, added a few words to the first part of the Ninth Article, so that it reads: "Of Baptism, they teach that it is necessary to salvation, *as a ceremony instituted of Christ."* So far, at least, we think all could go in affirming its necessity. And with such mild expressions, even those who were most remote from the Melanchthonian spirit, were satisfied.

"Among all orthodox Lutherans (and never has there been a stricter orthodoxy than the Lutheran,) Hutter is the most orthodox; no one has remained so thoroughly within the bounds of the theology authorized and made normative by the Church than he—no one has adhered with more fidelity, not merely to the spirit, but to the very letter of the Symbols, especially of the Form of Concord."[196] Yet Hutter exhausts, in the following answer, the question: "Is Baptism necessary to salvation?" "It is; and that *because of God's* command. For whatever God has instituted and commanded, is to be done, is precious, useful and necessary, though as to its outward form it be viler than a straw."[197] So much and no more does this great Theologian say of the *necessity* of Baptism in his Compend. Later theologians have properly given prominence to its necessity as a *means,* but never have ascribed to it a necessity *per se.*

VII. Yet not Unconditionally.

For finally on this point, the Church never has held, but has ever repudiated the idea, that Baptism is *"unconditionally* essential" or necessary "to salvation."

She has limited the necessity, first of all, by the *"possibility* of having it"—has declared that it is not *absolutely* necessary, and that not the deprivation of Baptism, but the contempt of it condemns a man[198]—that though God binds us to the means, as the

---

[196] Herzog's Encyclop. fuer. Theol. VI. 346.
[197] Compendium Loc. XX. 3. This answer is taken from Luther's Larger Catechism.
[198] Leipz. Edit. XXII. 400—422.

ordinary instruments of His grace, He is not Himself limited by them.[199] She teaches, moreover, that all the blessings of baptism are conditioned on faith.— C. M., 490: 33—36.

The "Shorter Catechism" of Luther, which our General Synod has issued, and authorized as a manual for training our children in the knowledge of the Gospel, teaches us that whatever Baptism gives, it gives alone to those "who believe that which the Word and promises of God assure us of." "The Water cannot do such a great thing, but it is done by the Word of God, and faith which believes the Word of God, added to the water." We shall not give the reference for this, as even the little children are supposed to know it by heart, nor stultify ourselves or our readers by adducing authorities for the catechetical doctrines of our Church.

The Judgment Of The Lutheran Church further Illustrated.

The Lutheran Church, holds that Baptism is necessary to salvation, inasmuch as God has commanded it, and obedience to his commands, is necessary to salvation; and, furthermore, because he has appointed Baptism, as one ordinary and positive channel of his grace, through which channel we are to seek the grace it offers. But our Church denies, that, where the command cannot be carried out, because of a necessity of God's creating, the lack of the sacrament involves the loss of the soul.

Luther.

On this question, the language of Luther is very explicit. In his "Christliche Bedencken," published in 1542,[200] in reply to the anxious questions of Christian

---

[199] Do. p. 412.
[200] Leipz. Ed. p. 418.

mothers, he rebukes and forbids the superstitious practice of the Romish Church, of baptizing a child not fully born—a practice based upon the idea, of the absolute necessity of baptism, to the Salvation of a child, and which would find some justification in that theory.

He directs, that those who are present, shall hold firmly to Christ's words: "Unless a man be born again, he cannot enter the kingdom of God," and shall kneel down, and, in faith, pray that the Lord will make this (unbaptized) child, partaker in his sufferings and death, and shall *then not doubt,* that He knows full well how, according to his divine grace and pity, to fulfil that prayer.

Wherefore, since the little child (unbaptized) has, by our earnest prayer, been brought to Christ, and this prayer has been uttered in faith, what we beg, is established with God, and heard of him, and he gladly receiveth it (the child :) as he himself says, Mark 10:14: "Suffer little children to come unto me, and forbid them not: for of such is the kingdom of God." Then should we hold that the little child, though it has not obtained Baptism, is not on that account lost, *("das Kindlein, ob es wohl die rechte Taufe nicht erlanget, davon nicht verlohren ist.")* There are several other passages in Luther, bearing on the same subject, but what we have given is ample.

Bugenhagen,

This "Bedencken" of Luther, was accompanied by an Exposition of the twenty-ninth Psalm, by Bugenhagen, (Pomeranus,) which Luther endorses. The main object of Bugenhagen, in the Treatise, is to give consolation in regard to unbaptized children, over against, what he styles, "the shameful error, drawn not from God's Word, but from man's dreams, that such children are lost." Bugenhagen, [201] after teaching parents to commit to God, in prayer, their child which cannot be baptized, adds: "This shall we *assuredly believe,* that Christ receives the child, and we should not commit it to the secret judgment of God. To commit it to the secret judgment of God, is to throw to the wind, and despise the promises in regard to little children." Both Luther and Bugenhagen discuss, at large, the arguments for, and the objections against, the doctrine of the salvation of unbaptized children, and demonstrate that it is no part of the faith of our Church, that Baptism is *absolutely* necessary; that is, that there are no *exceptions* nor *limitations* to the proposition, that, unless a man be born again, of water or Baptism, he cannot enter the kingdom of God.

LUTHER AND BUGENHAGEN condemn those who refuse to unbaptized children the rites of Christian burial, and who object to lay their bodies in consecrated ground, as if they were outside of the Church. "We bury them," say they, "as Christians, confessing, thereby, that we believe the strong assurance of Christ," "The bodies of these (unbaptized) children, have part in the joyous Resurrection—the Resurrection of life." GERHARD, and all our theologians, so, far as we are aware, without an exception, present and argue for the same views,

Hoffman.

Hoffman, (Tübingen, 1727,) to whom we owe one of the most admirable of the older Expositions of the Confession, says :[202] "It does not follow, from these words, (not born again of Baptism,) that all children of unbelievers, born out of the Church, are lost. Still less, is such an inference true, of the *unbaptized* infants of

---

[201] Do. p. 412.
[202] Pp. 36, 37.

Christians, For, although Regeneration is ordinarily wrought in infants by Baptism, yet it may be wrought, extraordinarily, by an operation of the Holy Spirit, without means, which the Augsburg Confession does not deny in these words. It merely desires to teach the absolute necessity of the new birth, or regeneration, and the ordinary necessity of Baptism. On the question, whether the infants of the heathen nations are lost, most of our theologians prefer to *suspend their judgment.* To affirm, as a certain thing, that they are lost, could not be done without rashness."

Fuerlin.

Fuerlin says :[203] "In regard to the infants of unbelievers, we are either to suspend our judgment, or adopt the milder opinion, in view of the universality of the grace of Christ, which can be applied to them, by some extraordinary mode of regeneration."

Our Theologians in general. Cotta,

On the more difficult question, whether infants born out of the Church, are saved, many of our old divines, of the strictest school, have maintained that it would be harsh and cruel, to give over, absolutely, to condemnation, the infants of pagans, for the lack of that which it was impossible for them to have, This view has been defended at large, by Dannhauer, Hulsemann, Scherzer, J. A. Osiander, Wagner, Musaeus, Spener, and very many others. Some of our best theologians, who have not considered the argument on either side, as decisive, have suspended their judgment in the case, as did Gerhard, Calixtus, Meisner, Baldwin, Bechman, and others. HUNNIUS, whom Gerhard quotes approvingly, makes the statement of this middle view,

---

[203] Bechmann, Annotat in Hutt. Compend., p. 658.

in these words: "That the infants of pagans are saved, outside of the Church, is a matter on which the silence of Scripture forbids us to pronounce with assurance on the one side, yet, I would not dare to affirm, on the other, that those little ones, without distinction are lost,

For, 1. Since God desires the death of none, absolutely, it cannot rightly be supposed that he takes pleasure in the death of these little ones. 2. Christ died for them also. 3. They are necessarily excluded from the use of the Sacraments. Nor will God visit the children with eternal death, on account of the impiety of the parents, Ezek. 18. We commit them, therefore, to the decision of God."

COTTA approves of the most hopeful view of their condition, and argues for it—1. "From the infinite pity of God; 2. The extent of the benefits wrought by Christ; 3. The analogy of faith—no one is absolutely reprobated, but actual unbelief alone condemns; 4. Not the absence, but the contempt of Baptism condemns; 5. God can operate in an extraordinary way; 6. Though original sin, *in itself,* merits damnation, and is a *sufficient* cause of it, yet it is not (because of God's *infinite goodness*) an *adequate* cause of the actual infliction of that condemnation."[204]

IX. What, then, is Baptism? and what are its Blessings?

By Christian Baptism our Church understands not mere water (Cat. Min. 361, 2,) but the whole divine institution, (Cat. Maj. 491, 38—40) resting on the command of the Savior, Matt. 28:19, (Cat. Min. 361, 2,) in which he comprehends, and with which he offers the promise, Mark 15:15., (Cat. Min. 362, 8,) and which is, therefore, ordinarily necessary to salvation, (Aug. Conf. II, 2; IX, 1, 3,) in which institution, water (whether by

---

[204] Calovius Bibl. Illustrat. iv, 552.

immersion, Cat. Maj. 495, 65, sprinkling or pouring, Cat. Maj. 492, 45) applied by a minister of the gospel (Aug. Conf. V, 1 and XIV,) in the name of the Trinity, (Cat. Min. 361, 4,) to adults or infants, (Aug. Conf. IX, 2,) is not merely the sign of our profession, or of our actual recognition as Christians, but is rather a sign and testimony of the will of God toward us (A. C. XIII,) offering us his grace, (do. IX) and not *ex opere operato* (do. XIII, 3,) but in those only who rightly use it, that is, who believe from the heart the promises which are offered and shown, (A.C. XIII, 2; Cat Maj. 490, 33,) is one of the instruments whereby the Holy Spirit is given (A. C. V, 2,) who excites and confirms faith, whereby we are justified before God (A.C.V. 3,) so that they who thus receive, or use it, are in God's favor, (A. C. IX, 2,) have remission of their sins, (Nic. Creed 9,) are born again (A. C. II, 2,) and are released from condemnation and eternal death, (A. C. II, 2; Cat. Min. 361, 6,) so long as they are in a state of faith, and bring forth holy works, (Aug. Conf. Art. XIII, 1, 6, Cat. Min. 362, 11—14,) while, on the other hand, where there is no faith, a bare and fruitless sign, so far as benefit to the soul is concerned, alone remains (Cat. Maj. 496, 73,) and they who do not use their Baptism aright, and are acting against conscience, letting sin reign in them, and thus lose the Holy Spirit, are in condemnation from which they cannot escape, except by true conversion; (A. C. XIII,) a renewal of the understanding, will and heart; (Cat. Maj. 496, 68, 69; Form. Conc. 605, 70.)

This is the doctrine of our Church, and not one letter of it is destitute of the sure warrant of God's Eternal Word.

The intelligent examiner will soon discover, that while the whole sum and tendency of the *Romish* and *Romanizing* doctrine of the Sacraments, is to make them a *substitute for faith* in the justification of man, the doctrine of the Lutheran Church, in consonance with Holy Scripture, makes them a guard and bulwark of the glorious central truth, that "by grace we are saved, through faith; and that, not of ourselves, it is the gift of God." Her view of the nature of the efficacy of the Word and Sacraments, is the only one which solves the question: How God can be *Sovereign,* and yet *man* be accountable, and how the Church can at once avoid the perilous extreme of Pelagianism, on the one hand, and of Calvinism on the other.

X. Baptismal Regeneration.

The facts we have dwelt upon dispose of another charge against our Church—the charge of teaching an unscriptural doctrine in regard to regeneration, and the relation of Baptism to it.

The definite Platform (p. 29) says of "Baptismal Regeneration:" "By this designation is meant the doctrine that Baptism is necessarily and invariably attended by spiritual regeneration, and that such *water* Baptism is *unconditionally* essential to salvation." "Regeneration, in its proper sense of the term, consists in a radical change in our religious views — in our religious feelings, purposes, habits of action." Do., p. 30. The Miami Synod, in 1858, set forth what they supposed to be meant by the charge, when "they utterly repudiate and abhor" (as well they may) the following error: "Baptismal Regeneration—that is, that Baptism is necessarily connected with, or attended by, an internal spiritual change *ex opere operato,* or from the mere outward performance of the act." *(Luth. Observ. XXVI, 29.)* Their definition and that of the Platform, are substantially the same; though we do not understand them to charge such a doctrine upon their Church or its Confession.

The charge against our Church of teaching "Baptismal Regeneration," as those who make the charge define it, is, as we have seen, utterly ungrounded. It is not true in its general statement nor in its details; it is utterly without warrant in the whole, or in a single particular.

THE COUNTER-THEORY OF BAPTISM.

We have presented a few facts in elucidation and defense of the Scripture doctrine of Baptism, as confessed by our Church, and as misrepresented and assailed in the Definite Platform. It is always an interesting question, often a very important one. If we give up that which is assailed, what shall we have in the place of it? This question is of great importance in the present case. What equivalent do those propose to the Church, who ask her to give up her most cherished doctrines?

I. Baptism of Adults. The Confession and the Platform Compared.

What is the doctrine which the Definite Platform proposes as the true one, in place of that theory of "Baptismal Regeneration" which it denounces? It is this, (p. 30,) "Baptism in adults, is *a pledge* and CONDITION of obtaining those blessings purchased by Christ, and offered to all who repent, believe in Him, and profess his name by Baptism."

Now is not that which is a CONDITION of obtaining a thing, necessary to it—and is not "salvation" the generic term for the "blessings purchased by Christ?" How, then, can the Platform take offence at the ninth Article of our Confession. Just put them side by side?

Aug. Conf.: Baptism	is necessary	to salvation.
Def. Plat.: Baptism	is a *condition*	those blessings
purchased	of obtaining	by Christ.

II. Baptism of Infants.

Then comes the question of the Baptism of *infants*. What here is the view which is to supersede that annihilated theory (if that may be said annihilated which never existed) "that Baptism is a *converting ordinance* in infants."

The theory is this, (p. 31): "'Baptism, in infants, is the *pledge of the bestowment* of those blessings purchased by Christ, for all. These blessings are, forgiveness of sins, or exemption from the penal consequences of natural depravity (which would at least be exclusion from heaven) on account of moral disqualification for admission," &c.

Look now at this and compare it with what our Confession says on the Baptism of *Infants*. (Art. IX.) All that it says on the subject is,

1. "That children are to be baptized." Here the Platform assents fully.

2. "That by this Baptism they are offered and committed to God."

Here, too, we apprehend, there will be no dissent, for Dr. S. says: "Baptism in infants, is the pledge of reception into the visible Church of Christ, grace to help in every time of need;"

3. "Being offered in Baptism to God, they are well-pleasing to God, (that is,) are received into the favor of God," says the Confession, and here it ceases to define the blessings of Baptism; but the Platform goes much further. "Baptism in infants," it says, "is a pledge." The first blessing of which it declares it to be a pledge, is "forgiveness of sins," conceding this, that infants have sins; that they need the forgiveness of sins; that *baptized infants* have the *pledge* of the forgiveness of their sins, and, of necessary consequence, that *unbaptized* infants have no pledge of the forgiveness of *their* sins; in other words, that there is no *pledge* that the sins of unbaptized infants are forgiven; for if they

have the pledge too, though they have no Baptism, how can Baptism be the pledge of forgiveness?

The words that follow now, are explanatory of the preceding ones. "These blessings are forgiveness of sins, or exemption from the penal consequences of natural depravity." Forgiveness is defined to be "exemption from penal consequences." Sins are defined to be "natural depravity."

Now wherein does this doctrine differ from the old one, that in Baptism the *"reatus,"* or liability of original sin is taken away, although the *"material"* remains? (Apolog. Confess., 83, 35.) Except, perhaps, in this, That Luther supposes God graciously to do it by his Holy Spirit *through* the Baptism, while the Platform may mean, that Baptism is only the *pledge* that it is done, but it is done either way, and in both—Baptism is the proof, at least, that it is done.

But we have, furthermore, a statement of what "the penal consequences of natural depravity" are: "Which would, at least, be *exclusion* from *heaven,* on account of moral disqualification for admission."

Now analyze this proposition, and you have the following result:

1. That infants have natural depravity, which is a moral disqualification for heaven.

2. That this *natural depravity has penal consequences,* that is, is a *punishable thing;* that infants, *consequently, have moral character,* and some sort of *moral accountability;* are the subjects of law, as to its obligation, for they have sins to be forgiven; and of law as to *its pains,* for they are subject to "penal consequences."

3. That this punishment would be exclusion from heaven. But this statement is qualified in a very remarkable way— "would, *at least,* be exclusion from heaven,"—that is the *minimum.* The words *"at least"* seem to mark this train of thought: "They would *at*

least be excluded from heaven, even if they were not sent to hell." Now this style of thinking, as it has in it, unconsciously to its author, we trust and believe—as it has in it a tinge of Pelagianism—so it trembles, logically, upon the very border of that figment to which the Pelagianism of the Church of Rome, combined with her strong sacramentalism, leads her—the doctrine of a *limbus infantum.* She was too *sacramental* to admit that the original sin of a child could be removed without Baptism; too Pelagian to concede that original sin must, in its own nature, apart from God's grace, *bring death* eternal. Her *sacramentalism,* therefore, kept the *unbaptized child out of heaven ;* her *Pelagianism kept it out of hell,* and the conjunction of the two generated a *tertium quid*—the fancy of a *"Limbus infantum,"* or place, which, without being hell, was yet one of exclusion from heaven, a mild perdition, whereby infants not wholly saved, were, nevertheless, not totally lost. And the shadow of this very tendency, shows itself in the words we have quoted from the Platform.

Connecting the three propositions now, with what has preceded them, we reach then, furthermore,

4. That God grants forgiveness of the sins of the baptized infant, forgives its natural depravity, exempts it, of course, from the penal consequences thereof, and thus, if it is not saved from a liability to eternal death, it is, *"at least,"* saved from exclusion from heaven. If the Platform means that the sin of an infant, unforgiven, would bring eternal death to it, then it goes as far as the extremest views of the nature of original sin can go, and vindicates the very strongest expressions of the Confession on this point; and if it means that original sin would exclude it from heaven without consigning it to despair, it has virtually the doctrine of the *limbus infantum.*

5. And finally, Baptism in infants is the pledge of all this,— they have the *pledge*—and, of consequence,

unbaptized infants have not. In other words, there is an *assurance* that every baptized child has this great thing, "forgiveness of sins."

It is not surprising that, after all this, the Platform closes its discussion on this point with these words, (p. 31): "It is proper to remark that the greater part of the passages in the former Symbols, relating to this subject, are, and doubtless *may be* explained by many, to signify NO MORE THAN WE ABOVE INCULCATE." We understand the author in this to concede, not simply that they are so explained, but that they are, in fact, susceptible of this explanation, and that this *may be* really their meaning.

It is our sincere belief, that if the energy which has been expended in assailing as doctrine taught by our Consessions, what they do not teach, had been devoted to ascertaining what is their real meaning, that these years of sad controversy would have been years of building up, and of closer union, not years of conflict, years in which our ministry and members have had their minds poisoned against the truth of God as held in our Church.

But, while there are apparent points of identity with the Church doctrine in that of the Platform, there is one *terrific chasm* in its theory, which nothing can bridge over. A contradiction of the most palpable and fatal character.

That vital defect is this, that while this theory secures the *forgiveness* of an infant's sins, it makes no provision whatever for the *change* of its sinful nature. While it provides for its *exemption* from *penalty,* it leaves utterly out of sight the *correction* of its depravity, which is a more fearful thing than the penalty which follows it; for in the pure judgment of sanctified reason, it would be better to be holy and yet bear the penalty of sin, than to be sinful and have the immunities of holiness; better to be sinless, although in hell, than to be polluted and in heaven.

The theory concedes that there is in "infants a *moral disqualification* for heaven." It absolutely needs, therefore, before an infant can have a *pledge* in Baptism of its salvation, that there shall be a pledge provided for its moral qualification for heaven, and this moral qualification must be REGENERATION.

But the theory not only does not provide for this, but as far as it is stated in the Platform, absolutely excludes it. It says, "Baptism in infants is a pledge of the forgiveness of sins," but it says not a word of their *removal* in whole or in part.

The cardinal defect is, that it provides a pledge that the *blessings which follow regeneration* shall be given, but none that the regeneration itself shall be given—that the child shall be saved from the *penalty* of sin without being saved, in whole or in part, from *the sin itself;* saved in fact *in* its sins, not *from* them. To what end would a child enter heaven if its nature were unchanged. *Forgiving* a sin in no sense changes the character. And where in the word of God is there the shadow of that baleful doctrine, that *the sins of an unregenerate person are forgiven*; where the shadow of that deadly error, that God has provided a Church, into which, *by his own ordinance, and at his command,* millions are brought, without *any change* in a nature whose moral evil is such as would condemn them forever to exclusion from heaven—where is the shadow of that fatal delusion, that the curse of sin can be removed while the sin itself remains dominant?

But if a refuge is sought in saying that infants are regenerated, but that Baptism, in all its parts, element, word and spirit, is not the ordinary channel of this grace, is to accept; a theory which has every difficulty which carnal reason urges against the doctrine of the Church, but which has nothing that even looks like a warrant for it in God's Word, and which, run out logically, would destroy the whole character of Christianity as a system of wonderful means to beneficent ends.

Calvinistic And Lutheran Views Of BAPTISM Compared.

Dr. Heppe, in his Dogmatik of the Evangelical Reformed Church, (1861,) presents the doctrines of the Calvinistic Churches, and illustrates his text with-citations from their *standard theologians.* The doctrine of the Lutheran Church, in regard to Baptism, is often very severely spoken of by Calvinists—it is, indeed, one of the main points of attack. Perhaps it may not be without some interest to compare the Lutheran and Calvinistic views, in regard to this important subject, on a few points.

The definitions of Baptism which Heppe gives as purely Calvinistic and Reformed, are as follows: "Baptism is a Sacrament, in which those *to whom the covenant of God's grace pertains,* are washed with water in the name of the Father, Son, and Holy Spirit, that is, that to those who are baptized, it is *signified and sealed,* that they are received into the *communion* of the covenant of grace, *are inserted into Christ,* and his mystic body, the Church, are *justified* by God, for the sake of Christ's blood shed for us, and *regenerated* by Christ's Spirit." This definition he gives from POLANUS. Another and shorter one he furnishes from WOLLEBIUS as follows: "Baptism is the first sacrament of the new covenant, in which *to the elect* received into the family of God, by the outward application of water, *the remission of sins and regeneration by the blood of Christ and by the Holy Spirit art sealed."* He gives only one other, which is from HEIDEGGER, thus: "Baptism is *the sacrament of regeneration, in which to each and to every one embraced in the covenant of God, the inward washing from sins through the blood and Spirit of Christ,* is declared *and sealed.*

This doctrine thus stated, and correctly stated, for it is the doctrine of all genuine Calvinists, involves several things, which the detractors of our Church may do well to ponder. First, It draws a line between baptized *infants* as well as between baptized *adults,* representing some as belonging to the elect, some to the non-elect, some as belonging to the class to whom the covenant of grace pertains, others as not of that class. Will Lutherans prefer this part of the doctrine to that of their own Church, which teaches them that God is the Father of all, and Christ the Savior of all, heartily loving all and desiring to save them? Will a *Lutheran mother* believe that it is *possible* that between her two beloved little children prattling at her knee, there may be, in *God's love, will and purpose, a chasm cleft back into eternity, and running down to the bottom of hell?* Can she believe this when her conscience tells her that the slightest *partiality on her part,* for the one or the other, would be a crime? Can she believe that God's absolute sovereignty elects absolutely one of her children to eternal glory, and passes by the other, when that passing by necessarily involves its ruin forever? Can Lutherans wonder that High Calvinism has been the mother of Universalism—that men who start with the premise, that the absolute sovereignty of God determines the eternal estate of men, should draw the inference, not that he elects *some* to life, and leaves the mass to go to perdition, but that he elects *all?* Will Lutherans give up this part of the baptismal doctrine of their Church? And yet if we surrender it—if we say the doctrine of Baptism is not a fundamental one in our system, men may teach among us on this point what they please. Who is to prevent these fearful views from being preached in our pulpits and taught in our houses?

A second feature of the Calvinistic view of Baptism is, that *to those perfectly alike in all personal*

respects, Bap*tism comes with entirely different functions.*
To one infant it signs and seals *communion in the*
covenant, insertion into Christ, justification and
regeneration; to another, perfectly alike in all personal
respects, it signifies and seals *nothing.* No parent knows
what his child receives in Baptism, whether it be a mere
handful of water on its hair, or the seal of blessings,
infinite like God, and irrevocable to all eternity. The
minister does not know what he has done; whether he
has sealed the everlasting covenant of God with an
immortal soul, or thrown away time and breath in
uttering mocking words, to that little being which
smiles and prattles, in utter unconsciousness that it is
abandoned to a destiny of endless pain, of unspeakable
horror. Can we give up the baptismal doctrine of our
Church for this? Our Church tells us that Baptism
makes the offer of the same blessing to every human
creature who receives it; that a difference in the result
of Baptism depends upon no lack of the divine grace,
on no secret council of God, but upon the voluntary
differences of adults—and that as there are no such
differences in infants, there is no difference in the
effects of Baptism to them. Surely Lutherans should
stand shoulder to shoulder in this, that whatever be the
blessing of Baptism, be it little or great, vague or
well-defined, it is offered alike to all, and *conferred* alike
upon all who do not present in themselves the
voluntary barrier to its reception. Yet if we say the
doctrine of Baptism is non-fundamental, these very
errors we abhor, may be set forth in our theological
chairs, taught in our Catechism, and set forth in our
pulpits.

A third element of the Calvinistic doctrine of
Baptism is, that to those for whom any of the blessings
of Baptism are designed, it supposes the sealing of as
great blessings, as on the strongest sacramental theory,
even that of the Church of Rome herself, is conferred

by Baptism; it seals to the elect, to whom alone its blessings belongs, reception into the "communion, that is the fellowship in, the participation in, the covenant of grace," "insertion into Christ and his mystic body," "justification," "regeneration," and "the inward washing of sin." Let Lutherans remember that it is here conceded that the highest blessings which our Church teaches us are connected alone with a *worthy* entrance into the baptismal covenant, and a *faithful continuance* therein, are acknowledged by Calvinists to be actually *sealed* therein—that is, that God sets his hand to it, by the act of baptizing, that the elect do *then* have, or shall *yet* have, if they have not then, justification, regeneration, and inward washing from sin. Shall we take offence at the doctrine of our Church, which asks us to receive as an article of faith, in regard to the efficacy of Baptism, no more than is summed up in the words of our Confession, that "through Baptism the grace of God is offered, that *children* are to be baptized, and being through Baptism offered to God, are received into his favor?"

Here, then, we rest the case. The doctrine of Baptism held and confessed by the Evangelical Lutheran Church is as all her doctrines are, absolutely accordant in every part with the Word of God. To abide by her Confession, is to abide by the Word, and there she and her true children will rest. If we destroy the historical life of our Church, and abandon her Confession, whither can we go? What system can we accept which will meet so fully our wants? If we destroy or rend the Lutheran Church, or allow as normal and final just as much deviation, as the individual may wish, from alt to which she has been pledged in her history, from all that is involved in her very name, from all that gave distinctive being, what may we hope to establish in her place to justify so fearful an experiment, and to indemnify the world for so great a loss?

www.ingramcontent.com/pod-product-compliance
Lightning Source LLC
Chambersburg PA
CBHW072005040426
42447CB00009B/1496